Table Of Contents

Chapter 1: Introduction to Digital Marketing

Understanding the Basics of Digital Marketing

Understanding the Basics of Digital Marketing

In today's fast-paced digital era, having a solid understanding of the basics of digital marketing is crucial for content creators, digital creators, and social media influencers. As a content creator, your success relies not only on creating compelling and engaging content but also on your ability to promote it effectively to reach a wider audience. This subchapter aims to provide you with an introduction to the fundamental concepts of digital marketing and how you can leverage them to enhance your online presence and grow your audience.

Digital marketing encompasses various strategies and techniques aimed at promoting products, services, or content through digital channels. It involves utilizing the internet, social media platforms, search engines, email marketing, and other online tools to reach and engage with your target audience. Understanding these key components will help you develop a comprehensive digital marketing strategy tailored to your niche.

One of the core aspects of digital marketing is search engine optimization (SEO). SEO involves optimizing your website, blog, or social media profiles to rank higher on search engine result pages organically. By incorporating relevant keywords, improving your website's loading speed, and enhancing user experience, you can increase your online visibility and drive more traffic to your content.

Another crucial element is social media marketing. As a content creator, you should be well-versed in utilizing social media platforms such as Instagram, YouTube, TikTok, or Twitter to promote your content and engage with your audience. Understanding how to create compelling social media posts, leverage hashtags, and engage with your followers will significantly enhance your digital marketing efforts.

Furthermore, email marketing plays a vital role in building a strong relationship with your audience. By collecting email addresses from your website or social media platforms, you can send newsletters, updates, or exclusive content directly to your subscribers. This not only helps you stay connected with your audience but also increases the chances of generating repeat visits to your content.

Understanding the basics of digital marketing will enable you to implement strategies that align with your goals and achieve measurable results. By combining effective SEO techniques, leveraging social media platforms, and utilizing email marketing, you can enhance your online presence, increase your visibility, and ultimately grow your audience.

In the following chapters, we will delve deeper into each of these digital marketing strategies, providing you with practical tips, best practices, and case studies to help you master the art of digital marketing as a content creator, digital creator, or social media influencer in your specific niche.

What is Digital Marketing?

What is Digital Marketing?

In today's fast-paced digital era, understanding the concept of digital marketing is crucial for content creators, digital creators, and social media influencers. As a content creator, you possess the power to captivate and engage your audience, but without a solid knowledge of digital marketing, your efforts may fall short of their full potential.

Digital marketing refers to the use of various online channels and strategies to reach and connect with a target audience, promote products or services, and ultimately drive profitable action. It encompasses a wide range of activities, including search engine optimization (SEO), social media marketing, email marketing, content marketing, paid advertising, and more.

For content creators, digital marketing acts as a catalyst to amplify their content's reach, impact, and influence. By leveraging the power of digital marketing techniques, you can effectively promote your work, build a loyal community, and monetize your efforts.

One of the fundamental pillars of digital marketing is SEO. By optimizing your content for search engines, you increase its visibility in organic search results, attracting more traffic to your website or social media platforms. Understanding how search engines rank content and using relevant keywords strategically can significantly enhance your online presence.

Social media marketing is another vital aspect of digital marketing for content creators. Engaging with your audience on platforms like Facebook, Instagram, Twitter, and YouTube enables you to build a strong online community and foster meaningful connections. By leveraging social media analytics and targeted advertising, you can amplify your content's exposure and reach a wider audience.

Content marketing plays a pivotal role in digital marketing as well. Creating valuable, informative, and entertaining content allows you to establish yourself as an authority in your niche and build trust with your audience. Sharing your expertise through blog posts, videos, podcasts, or infographics not only attracts more viewers but also increases your chances of collaboration and sponsorship opportunities.

Paid advertising is also an essential part of digital marketing for content creators. Platforms like Google Ads, Facebook Ads, and YouTube Ads enable you to target specific demographics, maximize your visibility, and drive traffic to your content or website.

In conclusion, digital marketing is the art of leveraging online channels and strategies to promote, amplify, and monetize your content as a content creator, digital creator, or social media influencer. By mastering the various aspects of digital marketing, you can unlock your true potential, reach a wider audience, and achieve your goals in the digital realm.

Why is Digital Marketing Important for Content Creators?

Why is Digital Marketing Important for Content Creators?

In today's digital age, content creators have more opportunities than ever to showcase their talent and reach a wide audience. However, with the ever-increasing competition, it is crucial for content creators to have a solid digital marketing strategy in place. Digital marketing has become an essential tool for content creators to amplify their reach, engage with their audience, and ultimately, monetize their content.

One of the primary reasons why digital marketing is important for content creators is its ability to increase visibility. With millions of content pieces being published every day, it is easy for creators to get lost in the sea of information. Digital marketing techniques such as search engine optimization (SEO), social media marketing, and influencer collaborations can help content creators stand out from the crowd and gain more visibility. By optimizing their content for search engines and leveraging social media platforms, creators can reach a larger audience and attract more followers.

Moreover, digital marketing enables content creators to engage with their audience on a deeper level. Through social media channels, creators can interact with their followers, respond to comments, and build a community around their content. This engagement not only helps creators understand their audience's preferences and needs but also fosters a loyal fan base. By consistently engaging with their audience, content creators can build trust and credibility, which are essential for long-term success.

Additionally, digital marketing provides content creators with various monetization opportunities. By strategically implementing affiliate marketing, sponsored content, and brand collaborations, creators can generate income from their content. Digital marketing allows content creators to identify potential partnership opportunities, negotiate deals, and create mutually beneficial relationships with brands and advertisers. This diversification of revenue streams provides creators with financial stability and the freedom to focus on creating high-quality content.

In conclusion, digital marketing plays a pivotal role in the success of content creators. It helps them increase their visibility, engage with their audience, and monetize their content. With the ever-evolving digital landscape, it is essential for content creators to stay updated with the latest digital marketing trends and techniques. By mastering the art of digital marketing, content creators can unlock their full potential and make a lasting impact in their respective niches.

The Evolution of Digital Marketing

The Evolution of Digital Marketing

In today's fast-paced digital world, it is crucial for content creators, digital creators, and social media influencers to stay on top of the ever-evolving landscape of digital marketing. This subchapter aims to provide a comprehensive overview of the evolution of digital marketing, from its humble beginnings to the cutting-edge strategies and trends that dominate the industry today.

Digital marketing has come a long way since its inception. Initially, it primarily consisted of simple banner advertisements and basic email marketing campaigns. However, with the rapid advancements in technology and the proliferation of social media platforms, digital marketing has transformed into a dynamic and multi-faceted field.

One significant milestone in the evolution of digital marketing was the advent of search engine optimization (SEO). SEO revolutionized the way content creators and digital marketers approached online visibility. By optimizing websites and content for search engines, businesses could reach a wider audience and improve their organic rankings on search engine result pages.

The rise of social media platforms such as Facebook, Twitter, and Instagram marked another pivotal moment in digital marketing history. These platforms provided content creators and social media influencers with new avenues to engage with their audiences directly. Brands quickly recognized the power of influencer marketing, partnering with content creators to promote their products and services to a highly engaged and targeted audience.

As technology continued to advance, mobile marketing emerged as a game-changer in the digital marketing landscape. With the widespread adoption of smartphones, mobile marketing became essential for reaching consumers on the go. Mobile-responsive websites, mobile apps, and location-based advertising opened up a world of opportunities for content creators and digital marketers to connect with their audiences in real-time.

In recent years, the evolution of digital marketing has been heavily influenced by data analytics and automation. With the advent of sophisticated tools and platforms, content creators and digital marketers can now analyze vast amounts of data to gain insights into consumer behavior, preferences, and trends. This data-driven approach allows for more targeted and personalized marketing campaigns, leading to higher conversion rates and customer satisfaction.

In conclusion, the evolution of digital marketing has transformed the way content creators, digital creators, and social media influencers engage with their audiences. From basic banner ads to data-driven, personalized campaigns, the digital marketing landscape continues to evolve at a rapid pace. Staying abreast of the latest trends and strategies is crucial for success in this ever-changing field. By embracing new technologies and adopting innovative approaches, content creators and digital marketers can effectively navigate the digital landscape and achieve their goals.

Traditional Marketing vs. Digital Marketing

Traditional Marketing vs. Digital Marketing

In today's digital age, the world of marketing has undergone a significant transformation. Gone are the days when traditional marketing methods like print advertising, television commercials, and billboards ruled the industry. The rise of the internet and social media has given birth to a new era of marketing known as digital marketing, which has become the go-to strategy for many content creators, digital creators, and social media influencers.

So, what exactly is the difference between traditional marketing and digital marketing? Let's dive into this subchapter to explore the various aspects of both approaches and understand how content creators can leverage digital marketing to their advantage.

Traditional marketing refers to the conventional methods of promoting products or services through offline channels. This includes print advertisements in newspapers and magazines, television and radio commercials, direct mail campaigns, and outdoor advertising such as billboards and signage. While traditional marketing has been successful for many years, it often lacks the targeted reach and measurability that digital marketing can offer.

On the other hand, digital marketing encompasses all marketing efforts that leverage online channels, such as websites, social media platforms, search engines, email marketing, and mobile applications. The key advantage of digital marketing lies in its ability to target specific audiences, track and measure campaign performance, and engage with customers in real-time. With the power of data analytics and consumer insights, content creators can tailor their marketing strategies and content to reach the right audience at the right time.

Digital marketing offers a wide range of tools and tactics that content creators can utilize to enhance their online presence and engage with their audience. These include search engine optimization (SEO), social media marketing, content marketing, influencer collaborations, email marketing, and paid advertising. By leveraging these digital marketing strategies, content creators can build a strong brand, increase their reach, and drive traffic to their platforms.

It is important for content creators, digital creators, and social media influencers to consider both traditional and digital marketing approaches when developing their marketing strategies. While traditional marketing can still be effective in reaching certain demographics, digital marketing holds the key to unlocking a wider and more engaged audience. By embracing the power of digital marketing, content creators can stay ahead in this fast-paced digital landscape and maximize their chances of success.

In conclusion, traditional marketing and digital marketing each have their own merits. However, in the age of digital dominance, content creators, digital creators, and social media influencers must adapt and embrace the opportunities that digital marketing presents. By understanding the differences between these two approaches and leveraging the right digital marketing strategies, content creators can truly unlock their potential and thrive in the ever-evolving world of digital marketing.

The Rise of Digital Marketing in the Content Creation Industry

The Rise of Digital Marketing in the Content Creation Industry

In today's digital age, the content creation industry has experienced a significant shift due to the rise of digital marketing. As content creators, digital creators, and social media influencers, it is crucial to understand the impact and opportunities that digital marketing brings to our respective niches.

Digital marketing has revolutionized the way content is created, distributed, and consumed. It has provided content creators with an array of new platforms and tools to reach their target audience more effectively. With social media platforms like Instagram, YouTube, and TikTok, content creators now have the ability to engage with millions of followers instantaneously. The power of digital marketing has allowed individuals to transform their passions into profitable careers.

One of the key advantages of digital marketing for content creators is the ability to build and maintain a strong personal brand. Through strategic digital marketing techniques such as search engine optimization (SEO), social media advertising, and influencer collaborations, content creators can increase their online visibility and attract a larger audience. By consistently delivering high-quality content that aligns with their brand, content creators can establish themselves as industry experts and gain the trust and loyalty of their followers.

Furthermore, digital marketing offers content creators the opportunity to monetize their content in various ways. From sponsored posts and brand partnerships to affiliate marketing and product endorsements, content creators can generate income through collaborations with brands that align with their niche. The rise of digital marketing has created a vast marketplace where content creators can connect with brands and negotiate mutually beneficial partnerships.

However, with the increased competition in the digital space, it is essential for content creators to stay updated with the latest digital marketing trends and strategies. By investing time and effort in learning about search engine algorithms, social media algorithms, and consumer behavior, content creators can optimize their content for maximum visibility and engagement.

In conclusion, the rise of digital marketing in the content creation industry has transformed the way we create, distribute, and monetize content. As content creators, digital creators, and social media influencers, embracing digital marketing techniques is crucial to building a successful personal brand, attracting a larger audience, and monetizing our content effectively. By staying informed and adapting to the ever-evolving digital landscape, we can leverage the power of digital marketing to thrive in our respective niches.

Chapter 2: Building a Strong Digital Presence

Creating a Brand Identity

Creating a Brand Identity

In the ever-evolving world of digital marketing, content creators, digital creators, and social media influencers play a crucial role in shaping brand identities. As a content creator, your brand identity is what sets you apart from the competition and establishes a strong connection with your audience. This subchapter explores the essential elements and strategies for creating a compelling brand identity that resonates with your target audience and helps you thrive in the realm of digital marketing.

First and foremost, understanding your target audience is paramount. You need to identify who your content is intended for and what they value. By delving deep into their preferences, interests, and pain points, you can tailor your content to meet their needs effectively. This insight will enable you to develop a brand identity that aligns with their desires, making it easier to build a loyal following.

Consistency is key when it comes to establishing a brand identity. Your audience should be able to recognize your content instantly, regardless of the platform they encounter it on. This means maintaining a cohesive visual aesthetic, tone of voice, and messaging across all your content channels. Consistency breeds familiarity, which strengthens your brand identity and fosters trust with your audience.

Another vital aspect of creating a brand identity is storytelling. Humans are inherently drawn to narratives, so crafting a compelling story around your content and brand can make a significant impact. Your story should resonate with your audience, evoke emotion, and demonstrate your values and unique selling proposition. Use your content to tell this story and create an emotional connection that goes beyond just the products or services you offer.

To further solidify your brand identity, consider incorporating branding elements such as a logo, color palette, and typography that reflect your brand's personality. These visual elements should be consistent across all your digital marketing efforts, including your website, social media profiles, and any promotional materials.

Finally, collaboration with other content creators and influencers in your niche can help you expand your reach and strengthen your brand identity. By partnering with like-minded individuals, you can tap into their audience and create content that resonates with both your communities. Collaborations also lend credibility and authority to your brand, helping you establish a stronger foothold in the digital marketing landscape.

Creating a brand identity as a content creator is an ongoing process. It requires continuous refinement, adaptation, and a deep understanding of your target audience. By staying true to your brand's values, consistently delivering high-quality content, and engaging with your audience, you can build a strong brand identity that sets you apart in the competitive world of digital marketing.

Defining Your Brand's Mission and Values

Defining Your Brand's Mission and Values

As a content creator, digital creator, or social media influencer in the fast-paced world of digital marketing, it is crucial to understand the importance of defining your brand's mission and values. In this subchapter, we will explore how to identify and establish a clear mission and values that align with your niche in digital marketing.

Your brand's mission serves as the guiding force behind your content creation. It defines the purpose of your brand and sets the tone for the messages you deliver to your audience. Without a well-defined mission, your content may lack direction and fail to resonate with your target audience.

To define your brand's mission, start by asking yourself a few fundamental questions. What is the purpose of your content? What value do you aim to provide to your audience? How do you want your brand to be perceived? Your mission should reflect your answers to these questions and encapsulate your unique selling proposition.

Once you have established your mission, it is equally important to define your brand's values. Your values represent the core principles and beliefs that guide your brand's behavior and decision-making. They serve as the foundation for building trust and establishing a genuine connection with your audience.

To determine your brand's values, consider the qualities and characteristics you want to be associated with. Do you prioritize transparency and authenticity? Are you committed to delivering high-quality and reliable information? By defining your values, you create a framework for consistent behavior and messaging across all your content.

When your audience understands your brand's mission and values, they are more likely to connect with your content and become loyal followers. Authenticity is highly valued in the digital marketing world, and having a clear mission and values helps you stand out among the vast sea of content creators.

Remember, your mission and values are not set in stone. As you grow and evolve as a content creator, it is natural for your brand's mission and values to evolve as well. Regularly reviewing and redefining them will ensure that your content remains relevant, resonates with your audience, and enables you to stay ahead in the ever-changing landscape of digital marketing.

In conclusion, defining your brand's mission and values is a critical step in establishing a strong foundation for your content creation. It helps you align your messaging, connect with your target audience, and build a loyal following. By understanding and embracing your mission and values, you position yourself as a reputable digital marketer in your niche.

Developing a Unique Brand Voice

Developing a Unique Brand Voice

In the fast-paced world of digital marketing, standing out from the crowd is essential for content creators, digital creators, and social media influencers. One of the most effective ways to achieve this is by developing a unique brand voice that resonates with your target audience. Your brand voice is the personality and tone of your content that sets you apart from competitors and creates a lasting impression on your audience.

To begin developing your brand voice, you must first understand your target audience. Who are they? What are their interests and pain points? By understanding your audience, you can better tailor your content to meet their needs and preferences. This deep understanding will allow you to create a brand voice that speaks directly to them, making your content more relatable and engaging.

Once you have a clear understanding of your audience, it's time to define your brand's personality. Are you fun and lighthearted? Or are you more serious and professional? Your brand personality should align with your target audience's values and resonate with them on an emotional level. This will help you build a strong connection with your audience and foster loyalty.

Consistency is key when developing a brand voice. Your brand voice should be consistent across all your digital marketing channels, including social media, blog posts, videos, and podcasts. This ensures that your audience recognizes your content and feels a sense of familiarity with your brand. Consistency also helps build trust and credibility, as it shows that you are reliable and committed to delivering value.

To truly make your brand voice unique, consider incorporating storytelling into your content. Storytelling allows you to connect with your audience on a deeper level and create a memorable experience. Whether it's sharing personal anecdotes, case studies, or success stories, storytelling adds a human touch to your content and helps your audience connect with your brand on an emotional level.

In conclusion, developing a unique brand voice is essential for content creators, digital creators, and social media influencers in the field of digital marketing. By understanding your audience, defining your brand's personality, and maintaining consistency, you can create a brand voice that stands out from the competition. Incorporating storytelling into your content further enhances your brand's uniqueness and fosters a lasting connection with your audience. Remember, your brand voice is an essential tool in building a successful digital marketing strategy, so invest the time and effort to develop a voice that truly represents your brand.

Optimizing Your Website and Blog

Subchapter: Optimizing Your Website and Blog

In the ever-evolving digital landscape, having a strong online presence is crucial for content creators, digital creators, and social media influencers. One of the key aspects of building a successful brand and reaching a wider audience is optimizing your website and blog. This subchapter will delve into the fundamental strategies and techniques to enhance your digital marketing efforts and maximize your online visibility.

1. Understanding SEO: Search Engine Optimization (SEO) is the backbone of any successful website or blog. Learn how search engines work, the importance of keywords, and how to incorporate them strategically in your content to increase organic traffic and improve search engine rankings.

2. Compelling Content: Quality content is king! Discover the art of crafting engaging, informative, and shareable content that resonates with your target audience. Learn how to optimize your headlines, meta descriptions, and tags to improve click-through rates and encourage social sharing.

3. Mobile Optimization: With the majority of internet users accessing content on mobile devices, it is crucial to ensure your website and blog are optimized for mobile viewing. Explore responsive design, page speed optimization, and mobile-friendly layouts to provide a seamless user experience across all devices.

4. Navigation and User Experience: Create a user-friendly website and blog by focusing on intuitive navigation, clear call-to-actions, and easy-to-find information. Learn how to structure your content, use relevant internal links, and optimize your site architecture to enhance user experience and reduce bounce rates.

5. Visual Appeal: Incorporate visually appealing elements such as images, videos, and infographics to engage your audience and make your content more shareable. Understand the importance of optimizing visual content for faster loading times and using alt tags for improved accessibility and SEO.

6. Analytics and Tracking: Implementing analytics tools, such as Google Analytics, allows you to track and measure your website's performance. Gain insights into user behavior, demographics, and traffic sources to make data-driven decisions and optimize your digital marketing strategies.

7. Social Media Integration: Integrate social media buttons, shareable content, and social media feeds into your website or blog to encourage audience engagement and expand your online presence. Learn how to leverage social media platforms to drive traffic and increase brand awareness.

By optimizing your website and blog, you can enhance your digital marketing efforts, improve your search engine rankings, and attract a larger audience. Remember, effective optimization is an ongoing process that requires continuous monitoring, analysis, and adaptation. Stay up-to-date with the latest trends and algorithms to ensure your website remains competitive in the dynamic world of digital marketing.

Understanding SEO for Content Creators

Understanding SEO for Content Creators

In today's digital landscape, where content creation has become a powerful tool for marketing, understanding SEO (Search Engine Optimization) is crucial for content creators. Whether you are a blogger, digital creator, or social media influencer, incorporating SEO strategies into your content can significantly boost your visibility, reach, and engagement. This subchapter aims to provide content creators with a comprehensive understanding of SEO and its significance in the digital marketing realm.

SEO is the process of optimizing your content to rank higher in search engine result pages (SERPs). By aligning your content with the algorithms used by search engines like Google, Bing, and Yahoo, you can improve your chances of appearing at the top of the search results. This increased visibility can drive organic traffic to your website, blog, or social media platforms, thereby expanding your audience and enhancing your digital presence.

To effectively implement SEO techniques, content creators must first understand the importance of keywords. Keywords are the words or phrases that users type into search engines to find specific information. By conducting thorough keyword research, content creators can identify the most relevant and high-traffic keywords for their niche. Incorporating these keywords strategically throughout their content, including titles, headings, meta descriptions, and body text, can help search engines recognize the relevance and quality of their content.

Additionally, content creators must optimize their content for mobile devices. With the increasing use of smartphones and tablets, mobile optimization has become an essential aspect of SEO. Ensuring that your website and content are mobile-friendly can improve user experience and increase your chances of ranking higher in mobile search results.

Furthermore, creating high-quality, informative, and engaging content is vital for SEO success. Search engines prioritize content that offers value to users. By producing content that addresses your audience's needs, answers their questions, or provides solutions to their problems, you can establish yourself as an authority in your niche and attract more organic traffic.

Lastly, content creators should embrace the power of backlinks. Backlinks are links from other websites that direct users to your content. These links act as votes of confidence for search engines, indicating that your content is valuable and trustworthy. Building a network of high-quality backlinks can improve your search engine rankings and increase your credibility as a content creator.

In conclusion, understanding SEO is essential for content creators in the digital marketing world. By optimizing your content with relevant keywords, focusing on mobile optimization, creating high-quality content, and building a network of backlinks, you can enhance your visibility, reach a wider audience, and ultimately achieve your digital marketing goals. Embrace the power of SEO and unlock the full potential of your content creation journey.

Crafting Engaging Web Content

Crafting Engaging Web Content

In today's digital age, creating engaging web content is crucial for content creators, digital creators, and social media influencers. The ability to captivate audiences and drive traffic to your website or social media platforms is what sets successful digital marketers apart. In this subchapter, we will explore the strategies and techniques necessary to craft compelling and captivating web content that resonates with your target audience.

1. Understanding Your Target Audience: The first step in creating engaging web content is understanding your target audience. Conduct thorough research to identify their demographics, interests, and pain points. This knowledge will help you tailor your content to their specific needs, ensuring it resonates with them on a deeper level.

2. Telling a Story: Crafting engaging web content involves telling a story. Humans are hardwired for storytelling, and by incorporating narratives into your content, you can create an emotional connection with your audience. Use vivid language, relatable anecdotes, and personal experiences to engage and captivate your audience from the start.

3. Utilizing Visuals: In the digital marketing world, visuals play a pivotal role in capturing attention. Incorporate high-quality images, videos, infographics, and other visually appealing elements into your web content. Visuals not only break up the text but also enhance the overall user experience, making your content more engaging and shareable.

4. Creating Valuable and Relevant Content: Engaging web content must provide value to your audience. Craft content that educates, entertains, or solves a problem for your target audience. Ensure your content is relevant to their interests and aligns with their needs and aspirations. By consistently delivering valuable content, you position yourself as an authority in your niche and build trust with your audience.

5. Encouraging Interaction and Conversation: Engaging web content should encourage interaction and conversation. Incorporate calls-to-action, such as asking your audience to leave comments, share their opinions, or participate in polls and surveys. Respond to comments promptly and engage with your audience to foster a sense of community and build a loyal following.

6. Optimizing for Search Engines: Crafting engaging web content goes hand in hand with search engine optimization (SEO). By optimizing your content for relevant keywords, you increase the chances of your web content appearing in search engine results. This drives organic traffic to your website and helps you reach a wider audience.

In conclusion, crafting engaging web content is a vital skill for content creators, digital creators, and social media influencers in the field of digital marketing. By understanding your target audience, telling a compelling story, utilizing visuals, creating valuable content, encouraging interaction, and optimizing for search engines, you can create web content that captivates, inspires, and drives results. Stay creative, stay relevant, and watch your audience grow.

Harnessing the Power of Social Media

Harnessing the Power of Social Media

In today's digital era, social media has become an integral part of our lives. It has revolutionized the way we connect, communicate, and consume content. For content creators, digital creators, and social media influencers, harnessing the power of social media is not just an option but a necessity to thrive in the competitive world of digital marketing.

Social media platforms offer a treasure trove of opportunities for content creators to reach and engage with their target audience. Whether you are a blogger, vlogger, podcaster, or any other type of content creator, it is crucial to understand how to leverage social media effectively to amplify your reach and grow your brand.

One of the key advantages of social media is its ability to provide instant feedback and engagement. By actively participating in conversations, responding to comments, and initiating discussions, content creators can build a loyal community of followers who feel connected to their work. This engagement not only helps in increasing brand visibility but also provides valuable insights into audience preferences and interests. By analyzing this data, content creators can refine their content strategy and create more compelling and relevant content that resonates with their audience.

Moreover, social media platforms offer a variety of tools and features to enhance your content's visibility. From hashtags to geotags, stories to live videos, these features allow you to showcase your content in creative and engaging ways. By understanding the algorithms and best practices of each platform, content creators can optimize their content for maximum visibility and reach.

Another aspect of harnessing the power of social media is influencer marketing. As a content creator, you have the opportunity to collaborate with brands and businesses to promote their products or services to your audience. By leveraging your influence and credibility, you can create sponsored content that seamlessly integrates with your regular content and provides value to your audience.

Finally, social media platforms also serve as a great source of inspiration and networking. By following industry leaders, fellow content creators, and relevant hashtags, you can stay updated with the latest trends, discover new ideas, and connect with like-minded individuals. Building a strong network within your niche can open doors to collaborations, partnerships, and growth opportunities.

In conclusion, social media has the power to transform your digital marketing efforts as a content creator. By actively engaging with your audience, optimizing your content, leveraging influencer marketing, and networking within your niche, you can harness the full potential of social media and take your content creation journey to new heights.

Choosing the Right Social Media Platforms

Choosing the Right Social Media Platforms

As a content creator, digital creator, or social media influencer in the realm of digital marketing, one of the most crucial decisions you will make is choosing the right social media platforms to showcase your content. With an overwhelming number of platforms available, each catering to different audiences and purposes, it is essential to make informed choices that align with your goals and target audience.

The first step in selecting the right social media platforms is understanding your niche within the digital marketing industry. Are you focusing on B2B or B2C marketing? Are you targeting a specific demographic or geographical location? By identifying your niche, you can narrow down the platforms that are most relevant to your audience.

One of the most popular social media platforms, Facebook, offers a wide reach and diverse user base. With its advanced targeting options and robust advertising capabilities, it is an excellent choice for content creators looking to engage with a broad audience. Additionally, Facebook groups provide an opportunity to connect with like-minded individuals and establish your expertise within your niche.

For visual content creators, Instagram and Pinterest offer unique opportunities to showcase your creativity. Instagram's highly visual nature and influencer-friendly environment make it an ideal platform for content creators in fashion, beauty, travel, and lifestyle niches. On the other hand, Pinterest's focus on inspiration and discovery is perfect for those in the home décor, DIY, or food industries.

If you are targeting a professional audience or offering B2B services, LinkedIn is the go-to platform. With its emphasis on networking and professional development, LinkedIn allows content creators to establish themselves as industry thought leaders and connect with potential clients or collaborators.

Twitter, with its fast-paced and real-time nature, is ideal for content creators who excel in short-form content and engaging with their audience through conversations and trending topics. Twitter is also an excellent platform for staying up-to-date with industry news and trends.

While these platforms are popular, it is crucial not to overlook emerging or niche platforms that may be more aligned with your target audience. Platforms like TikTok, Snapchat, or Twitch cater to younger demographics and offer unique opportunities for content creators who can adapt to their formats and engage with their communities.

In conclusion, choosing the right social media platforms as a content creator in the digital marketing industry requires considering your niche, target audience, and the unique features and benefits of each platform. By understanding your goals and the preferences of your audience, you can strategically select the platforms that will allow you to showcase your content, build a strong online presence, and ultimately achieve your digital marketing objectives.

Strategies for Building and Engaging Your Audience

Strategies for Building and Engaging Your Audience

As a content creator, digital creator, or social media influencer, one of your main objectives is to build and engage a loyal audience. After all, your success heavily relies on the number of followers, subscribers, and engaged viewers you have. In this subchapter, we will explore some effective strategies to help you achieve just that.

1. Define Your Target Audience: Before you start creating content, it's crucial to identify your target audience. Understand who they are, what they are interested in, their demographics, and their online habits. This will enable you to tailor your content to their specific needs and preferences.

2. Consistent Branding: Building a strong and recognizable brand is essential for attracting and retaining an audience. Create a consistent visual identity by using a specific color palette, fonts, and logos across all your platforms. This will help your audience easily recognize your content in a crowded digital space.

3. Quality Content Creation: Content is king, and creating high-quality, valuable content should be your top priority. Deliver content that educates, entertains, or inspires your audience. Invest time in research, planning, and editing to ensure your content stands out from the competition.

4. Utilize SEO Techniques: Search engine optimization (SEO) is crucial for increasing your visibility and reaching a wider audience. Conduct keyword research to understand what your target audience is searching for, and optimize your content accordingly. Incorporate relevant keywords, meta tags, and compelling headlines to improve your search engine ranking.

5. Engage with Your Audience: Building a relationship with your audience is key to retaining their loyalty. Engage with them through comments, direct messages, and social media polls. Respond to their queries, thank them for their support, and encourage them to share their thoughts and experiences. This will make them feel valued and connected to your brand.

6. Collaborate with Influencers: Collaborating with other content creators and influencers in your niche can be mutually beneficial. Partnering with influencers who have a similar target audience can help you expand your reach and gain credibility. Consider guest posting, co-creating content, or participating in joint campaigns to tap into new audiences.

7. Leverage Social Media: Social media platforms are powerful tools for building and engaging your audience. Choose the platforms that align with your target audience and focus your efforts there. Regularly post engaging content, interact with your followers, and utilize features like Instagram Stories, Facebook Live, or Twitter chats to create a sense of community.

Building and engaging your audience is an ongoing process that requires dedication, creativity, and adaptability. By implementing these strategies, you can effectively grow your digital presence, increase your reach, and foster a loyal community of followers and fans. Remember, your audience is the key to your success, so invest in nurturing and providing value to them.

Chapter 3: Content Strategy and Creation

Identifying Your Target Audience

Identifying Your Target Audience

In the ever-evolving world of digital marketing, understanding your target audience is paramount to the success of your content creation endeavors. As a content creator, digital creator, or social media influencer, knowing exactly who your audience is and how to effectively engage them is the key to achieving your goals and maximizing your impact.

One of the first steps in identifying your target audience is defining your niche within the realm of digital marketing. Whether you specialize in SEO strategies, social media marketing, email marketing, or any other area, it is crucial to understand where you fit in and what unique value you bring to the table. Defining your niche will not only help you stand out from the competition but also assist in determining who your target audience is.

Once you have identified your niche, it is time to delve deeper into understanding your target audience's characteristics, preferences, and behaviors. Conducting thorough market research will enable you to gather valuable insights that will inform your content creation strategies. Start by analyzing key demographic data such as age, gender, location, and occupation. This information will provide a foundation for crafting content that resonates with your audience on a personal level.

Beyond demographic data, it is essential to understand your target audience's psychographics. Psychographics delve into the psychological and emotional aspects of your audience, helping you uncover their values, interests, motivations, and pain points. By empathizing with your target audience's needs and desires, you can tailor your content to address their specific challenges and offer solutions that truly resonate.

Another effective way to identify your target audience is by analyzing your existing customer or follower base. Look for common patterns among your most engaged audience members. Are there specific demographics or psychographic traits that consistently stand out? Understanding the characteristics of your most loyal followers will allow you to attract similar individuals and build a strong community around your content.

Lastly, don't forget to leverage the power of analytics and data-driven insights. Platforms like Google Analytics, social media analytics, and email marketing metrics provide invaluable information about your audience's behavior, preferences, and engagement patterns. Utilizing these tools will help you fine-tune your content strategy and optimize your efforts to reach your target audience more effectively.

Identifying your target audience is a continuous process. As digital marketing trends evolve and new opportunities arise, it is crucial to stay attuned to the changing dynamics of your audience. Regularly revisit your audience profiles and make adjustments as needed to ensure your content remains relevant and impactful.

By investing time in understanding your target audience, you will be better equipped to create content that resonates, engages, and ultimately converts. Remember, your audience is at the heart of your digital marketing journey, and catering to their needs will be the driving force behind your success.

Conducting Market Research

Conducting Market Research

Market research is an essential step for content creators, digital creators, and social media influencers looking to succeed in the world of digital marketing. By understanding your target audience and the current market trends, you can create content that resonates with your audience and drives engagement. In this chapter, we will explore the various methods and tools you can use to conduct effective market research.

Understanding Your Target Audience:

Before creating any content, it is crucial to have a deep understanding of your target audience. Who are they? What are their interests? What challenges or problems do they face? By answering these questions, you can tailor your content to meet their needs and preferences. Start by conducting surveys, interviews, or focus groups to gain insights into your audience's preferences and behaviors.

Analyzing Competitors:

Analyzing your competitors can provide valuable insights into the market landscape. Identify your top competitors and research their content strategies, social media presence, and engagement levels. This analysis will allow you to identify gaps in the market and find opportunities to differentiate yourself. Additionally, pay attention to their audience engagement and feedback to gain a better understanding of what works and what doesn't.

Industry Trends and Keyword Research:

Staying up-to-date with the latest industry trends is crucial for content creators. Follow relevant blogs, news outlets, and social media channels to identify emerging topics and popular keywords. Conduct keyword research using tools like Google Trends or Keyword Planner to identify high-ranking keywords related to your niche. Incorporating these keywords into your content will improve its visibility and attract a larger audience.

Social Media Listening:

Social media platforms are a goldmine of consumer insights. Utilize social media listening tools to monitor conversations, mentions, and hashtags related to your niche. This will provide you with real-time feedback and allow you to gauge the sentiment around certain topics. By actively listening to your audience, you can adapt your content strategy to meet their changing needs and preferences.

Analyzing Data and Metrics:

Regularly analyze data and metrics to measure the effectiveness of your content. Use tools like Google Analytics, social media analytics, or email marketing analytics to track engagement, conversion rates, and audience demographics. This data will help you identify which content types and platforms are generating the most engagement, allowing you to refine your strategy accordingly.

In conclusion, conducting market research is vital for content creators, digital creators, and social media influencers. By understanding your target audience, analyzing competitors, staying updated on industry trends, utilizing social media listening, and analyzing data and metrics, you can create content that resonates with your audience and drives success in the digital marketing world.

Creating Audience Personas

Creating Audience Personas

One of the key elements in successful digital marketing is understanding your target audience. To effectively reach and engage with your audience, it's essential to create audience personas. An audience persona is a fictional representation of your ideal customer, which helps you tailor your content and marketing strategies to meet their specific needs and preferences.

As content creators, digital creators, and social media influencers, understanding your audience personas is crucial for creating content that resonates with your target market and drives engagement. By creating audience personas, you can gain valuable insights into your audience's demographics, interests, behaviors, and pain points, enabling you to deliver content that is relevant, valuable, and engaging.

To create audience personas, start by conducting thorough research. Dive deep into your analytics to understand who your current audience is and what content they engage with the most. Analyze their demographics, such as age, gender, location, and income level. Additionally, study their online behaviors, platforms they prefer, and the type of content they consume.

Once you've gathered this data, look for patterns and commonalities to identify different segments within your audience. These segments will serve as the basis for creating your audience personas. Give each persona a name and develop a detailed profile that includes their age, occupation, hobbies, goals, challenges, and preferred communication channels.

As you create audience personas, remember to keep them realistic and based on real data. Avoid making assumptions or generalizations, as this can lead to inaccurate representations of your target audience. Regularly update and refine your audience personas as you gain more insights and data about your audience.

Utilizing audience personas in your digital marketing strategy is highly beneficial. They provide a framework for creating content that speaks directly to your target audience's needs, interests, and pain points. By understanding your audience personas, you can craft compelling messages, tailor your content formats, and select the most effective marketing channels to reach and engage with your audience.

In conclusion, creating audience personas is essential for content creators, digital creators, and social media influencers in the niche of digital marketing. By investing time and effort in understanding your target audience, you can create content that resonates, builds trust, and drives meaningful connections with your audience, ultimately leading to a more successful digital marketing campaign.

Planning Your Content Calendar

Planning Your Content Calendar

In today's fast-paced digital world, creating high-quality content consistently is a crucial aspect of any successful digital marketing strategy. As content creators, digital creators, and social media influencers, you have the power to engage and captivate your audience through your unique content. However, it can be a challenging task to consistently come up with fresh ideas and ensure a steady stream of content. That's where a well-planned content calendar comes into play.

A content calendar is an essential tool for any content creator looking to stay organized and maintain a consistent content production schedule. It acts as a roadmap for your content creation journey, helping you plan and execute your digital marketing strategies effectively. Here are some key steps to consider when planning your content calendar:

1. Define Your Goals: Start by identifying your overarching goals for your digital marketing efforts. Whether it's increasing brand awareness, driving website traffic, or boosting conversions, having a clear objective will guide your content creation process.

2. Understand Your Audience: To create content that resonates with your target audience, it's crucial to have a deep understanding of their preferences, interests, and pain points. Conduct thorough research and gather insights about your audience to tailor your content accordingly.

3. Brainstorm Content Ideas: Set aside dedicated time for brainstorming content ideas. Consider the different types of content that align with your niche and audience, such as blog posts, videos, podcasts, or infographics. Think about what topics are trending in your industry and how you can provide unique value through your content.

4. Create a Content Calendar Template: Use a digital or physical calendar to create a framework for your content calendar. Break it down into monthly, weekly, or even daily slots, depending on the frequency of your content production. This template will serve as a visual representation of your content plan.

5. Plan Ahead: Allocate specific time slots for creating, editing, and publishing your content. Consider any upcoming events, holidays, or industry trends that you can leverage to create timely and relevant content.

6. Stay Consistent: Consistency is key when it comes to digital marketing. Stick to your content calendar as much as possible and ensure you deliver content on time. Engage with your audience regularly by responding to their comments, questions, and feedback.

By following these steps, you can effectively plan your content calendar and stay on top of your digital marketing efforts. Remember, a well-thought-out content calendar is not only a roadmap for your content creation journey but also a valuable tool for measuring your success and adjusting your strategies as needed. With careful planning and execution, your content can make a lasting impact on your audience and help you achieve your digital marketing goals.

Setting Goals and Objectives

Setting Goals and Objectives

In today's fast-paced digital world, content creators, digital creators, and social media influencers have become the driving force behind successful online businesses and brands. However, to truly thrive in this competitive landscape, it is essential to have a clear set of goals and objectives for your digital marketing efforts. This subchapter will guide you through the process of setting goals and objectives that align with your niche in digital marketing.

Effective goal setting is crucial for content creators as it provides direction, focus, and a roadmap for success. Without clearly defined goals, you may find yourself aimlessly creating content without any tangible results. By setting specific, measurable, attainable, relevant, and time-bound (SMART) goals, you can ensure that your efforts are purposeful and yield desired outcomes.

Firstly, it is important to define what you want to achieve with your digital marketing efforts. Are you aiming to increase your brand's visibility, drive more traffic to your website, or boost engagement on your social media platforms? Once you have a clear understanding of your objectives, you can start setting goals that will help you achieve them.

For example, if your objective is to increase your brand's visibility, a SMART goal could be to gain a certain number of followers on social media or to achieve a higher ranking on search engine results pages. These specific, measurable goals provide a benchmark against which you can track your progress and make necessary adjustments to your digital marketing strategy.

Furthermore, it is crucial to align your goals and objectives with your niche in digital marketing. Each niche has its own unique challenges and opportunities, so it is important to tailor your goals and strategies accordingly. For instance, if you are in the digital marketing niche, your goals may involve creating high-quality, informative content that positions you as an industry expert and attracts a target audience interested in learning about digital marketing strategies.

In conclusion, setting goals and objectives is a fundamental step in digital marketing for content creators, digital creators, and social media influencers. By establishing SMART goals that align with your niche, you can ensure that your efforts are purposeful, measurable, and effective. With a clear roadmap to success, you can take your digital marketing endeavors to new heights and achieve the online presence and success you desire.

Mapping Out Content Types and Topics

Mapping Out Content Types and Topics

As content creators, digital creators, and social media influencers in the world of digital marketing, it is crucial to have a well-thought-out plan for the types of content you create and the topics you cover. This subchapter aims to guide you through the process of mapping out your content types and topics, ensuring that your digital marketing efforts are focused, engaging, and effective.

First and foremost, understanding the different content types available to you is essential. From blog posts and videos to podcasts and social media posts, each content type presents unique opportunities to connect with your audience. Consider the strengths of each format and how they align with your goals. For instance, if you excel at delivering engaging visuals, focusing on video content might be the ideal choice. Alternatively, if you have a knack for writing and storytelling, investing in blog posts or long-form articles could be your path to success.

Once you have identified the content types that suit your strengths and resonate with your target audience, it's time to determine the topics you will cover. Start by considering your niche within the broad field of digital marketing. Are you an expert in social media marketing, SEO, or influencer marketing? Identify the specific areas within your niche that you excel in or have an interest in exploring further. This will help you refine your content focus and establish yourself as an authority in your chosen field.

While it's crucial to cover topics that align with your expertise, it's equally important to consider what your audience wants. Conduct thorough research to understand the pain points, challenges, and interests of your target audience. This will help you create content that provides value and addresses their needs, establishing you as a trusted resource in the digital marketing space.

Furthermore, it's beneficial to diversify your content topics to cater to different segments of your audience. Consider creating content for beginners, intermediate practitioners, and advanced professionals within your niche. This will allow you to engage with a wider range of individuals and build a loyal following.

Remember, mapping out your content types and topics is an ongoing process. Continuously assess the effectiveness of your content, track audience engagement, and adapt your strategy accordingly. By maintaining a flexible approach, you can stay ahead of trends, meet the evolving needs of your audience, and establish yourself as a leading content creator in the digital marketing landscape.

In conclusion, mapping out your content types and topics is a crucial step in your digital marketing journey. By understanding the strengths of different content formats, focusing on your niche, and addressing the needs of your audience, you can create engaging and impactful content that resonates with your target market. Stay adaptable, keep experimenting, and watch your digital marketing efforts flourish.

Crafting Compelling Content

Crafting Compelling Content

In the ever-evolving world of digital marketing, content creators hold the key to success. Their ability to engage and captivate audiences through compelling content is what sets them apart from the crowd. Whether you are a content creator, digital creator, or a social media influencer, mastering the art of crafting compelling content is crucial to your success in the field of digital marketing.

This subchapter aims to equip you with the knowledge and techniques needed to create content that resonates with your target audience, drives engagement, and ultimately leads to conversions. We will explore various aspects of crafting compelling content, including understanding your audience, storytelling techniques, and optimizing your content for digital platforms.

To begin with, understanding your audience is the first step towards crafting compelling content. By conducting thorough research and analysis, you can gain valuable insights into your target audience's preferences, interests, and pain points. This knowledge will enable you to tailor your content to meet their needs and effectively communicate your message.

Next, we delve into the power of storytelling. Humans have an innate affinity for stories, and incorporating storytelling techniques into your content can make it more relatable and memorable. By structuring your content around a compelling narrative, you can evoke emotions, create a connection, and leave a lasting impact on your audience.

Furthermore, optimizing your content for digital platforms is essential in today's digital marketing landscape. From SEO techniques to social media algorithms, understanding how these platforms function can significantly enhance the visibility and reach of your content. By employing relevant keywords, utilizing eye-catching visuals, and leveraging social media trends, you can ensure that your content reaches the right audience at the right time.

Finally, we explore the concept of consistency in content creation. Establishing a consistent brand voice, style, and publishing schedule will help you build a loyal following and maintain their engagement. Consistency also allows you to establish yourself as an authority in your niche and fosters trust with your audience.

In conclusion, crafting compelling content is not just about creativity; it is a strategic process that requires a deep understanding of your audience, storytelling techniques, and optimization for digital platforms. By incorporating these techniques into your content creation process, you can elevate your digital marketing efforts and stand out in the ever-growing digital landscape. So, grab your pen, unleash your creativity, and get ready to craft content that leaves a lasting impact!

Writing Engaging Blog Posts

Writing Engaging Blog Posts

In the world of digital marketing, content creators, digital creators, and social media influencers are constantly striving to create captivating and engaging blog posts. These blog posts serve as a powerful tool to attract and retain an audience, drive website traffic, and ultimately boost conversions. However, crafting blog posts that capture the attention of readers amidst the vast sea of online content can be a daunting task. This subchapter aims to provide content creators, digital creators, and social media influencers with practical tips and strategies to write irresistible blog posts that resonate with their target audience.

1. Know Your Audience: Before diving into writing a blog post, it is crucial to understand your target audience and their interests. Research their preferences, pain points, and the topics they are most likely to engage with. This will help you tailor your content to their needs and create a meaningful connection.

2. Create Catchy Headlines: A captivating headline is the first step towards drawing readers into your blog post. Craft a headline that is both informative and attention-grabbing. Use power words, numbers, or intriguing questions to entice readers and make them curious to explore your content further.

3. Tell a Story: Storytelling is a powerful technique to engage readers. Weave narratives into your blog posts that resonate with your audience's experiences and emotions. A compelling story will not only captivate readers but also make your content memorable and shareable.

4. Use Visuals: Incorporating eye-catching visuals such as images, infographics, or videos can significantly enhance the engagement level of your blog posts. Visual content not only breaks up the text but also captures attention, increases readability, and encourages social sharing.

5. Provide Value: Your blog posts should offer valuable information or insights to your audience. Focus on providing actionable tips, practical advice, or thought-provoking ideas that your readers can implement in their own lives. This will establish you as a trusted source and keep readers coming back for more.

6. Encourage Interaction: Engage with your audience by encouraging comments, questions, and sharing on your blog posts. Respond promptly to comments and foster conversations to create a sense of community. This will not only boost engagement but also provide valuable feedback and ideas for future content.

7. Optimize for SEO: Implementing basic search engine optimization (SEO) techniques will help your blog posts rank higher in search engine results and attract organic traffic. Use relevant keywords, optimize meta tags, and ensure your content is easily readable and shareable across different devices.

By following these tips, content creators, digital creators, and social media influencers can create blog posts that not only captivate their audience but also drive their digital marketing strategies forward. Remember, engaging blog posts have the power to establish you as an authority in your niche, build a loyal following, and ultimately contribute to the success of your digital marketing endeavors.

Creating Captivating Social Media Content

Creating Captivating Social Media Content

In today's digital age, social media has become an integral part of our lives. It has revolutionized the way we connect with others, share information, and even market our businesses. As content creators, digital creators, and social media influencers, understanding how to create captivating social media content is crucial to succeed in the ever-evolving world of digital marketing.

1. Know Your Audience: The first step in creating captivating social media content is to understand your audience. Dive deep into demographics, interests, and preferences of your target audience. This knowledge will help you craft content that resonates with them, making it more likely to engage and convert.

2. Storytelling: People love stories. Incorporate storytelling into your social media content to captivate your audience. Whether it's sharing personal experiences, behind-the-scenes glimpses, or success stories, storytelling adds a human touch and creates an emotional connection with your audience.

3. Visual Appeal: Social media is a visual platform, so make sure your content is visually appealing. Use high-quality images, videos, and graphics that are eye-catching and align with your brand's aesthetics. Experiment with different formats like carousels, infographics, and animations to add variety and keep your audience engaged.

4. Consistency is Key: Consistency in posting is crucial for building a loyal following. Develop a content calendar and stick to it. Regularly share valuable and engaging content to establish yourself as an authority in your niche. Consistency also helps in maintaining top-of-mind awareness among your audience.

5. Engage and Interact: Social media is all about connecting with your audience. Engage with your followers by responding to comments, messages, and mentions promptly. Show genuine interest in their opinions and feedback. This interaction not only strengthens your relationship with your audience but also enhances your credibility.

6. Experiment and Analyze: Don't be afraid to try new things on social media. Experiment with different types of content, hashtags, and posting times. Use analytics tools to track the performance of your posts and learn what works best for your audience. Adapt and refine your content strategy based on the insights gained.

7. Stay Up-to-Date: Digital marketing is an ever-evolving field. Stay updated with the latest trends, algorithms, and features of social media platforms. This knowledge will help you leverage new opportunities and stay ahead of your competitors.

Creating captivating social media content requires a combination of creativity, strategy, and understanding of your audience. By implementing these tips, you can enhance your digital marketing efforts, engage your followers, and achieve success as a content creator, digital creator, or social media influencer.

Chapter 4: Leveraging Email Marketing

Understanding the Power of Email Marketing

Understanding the Power of Email Marketing

In the ever-evolving digital landscape, content creators, digital creators, and social media influencers have become the driving force behind successful marketing campaigns. As a content creator, your ability to engage and connect with your audience is paramount. And one of the most effective ways to accomplish this is through email marketing.

Email marketing is a powerful tool that allows you to directly communicate with your audience, build trust, and nurture long-lasting relationships. It provides a platform for delivering targeted content, promotions, and updates right into the inbox of your subscribers. In this subchapter, we will dive into the ins and outs of email marketing and explore how it can revolutionize your digital marketing efforts.

First and foremost, email marketing allows you to personalize your message. By segmenting your subscribers based on their interests, preferences, and behaviors, you can create tailored content that resonates with them on a deeper level. This level of personalization not only boosts engagement but also increases conversions and sales.

Furthermore, email marketing enables you to stay top-of-mind with your audience. In the fast-paced world of digital marketing, where social media feeds are constantly updating, emails provide a more permanent and accessible channel for your content. By consistently delivering valuable and relevant information, you can establish yourself as an authority in your niche and keep your audience coming back for more.

Another key benefit of email marketing is the ability to track and measure your success. With powerful analytics tools, you can monitor open rates, click-through rates, and conversion rates. This data provides invaluable insights into the effectiveness of your campaigns, allowing you to make data-driven decisions and optimize your strategy for better results.

However, it's important to remember that effective email marketing goes beyond simply sending promotional emails. Building a strong connection with your audience requires providing value and solving their pain points. By offering exclusive content, insider tips, and valuable resources, you can position yourself as a trusted advisor and foster a loyal and engaged community.

In conclusion, understanding the power of email marketing is essential for any content creator, digital creator, or social media influencer looking to take their digital marketing efforts to new heights. By harnessing the personalization, durability, and analytics capabilities of email marketing, you can forge deeper connections with your audience, establish yourself as an authority, and drive tangible results for your business or brand.

Building an Email List

Building an Email List

In this digital age, where content creators, digital creators, and social media influencers are ruling the internet, one of the most effective ways to connect with your audience and build a loyal following is by building an email list. Whether you are a blogger, vlogger, or podcast host, having a strong email list is essential for your digital marketing success.

Why is an email list so important? Well, unlike social media platforms where your reach is limited by algorithms and changing trends, an email list gives you direct access to your audience's inbox. It allows you to establish a deeper connection with your followers and maintain constant communication.

So, how do you go about building an email list?

1. Create valuable content: The first step to attracting subscribers is by offering valuable content. Whether it's informative blog posts, entertaining videos, or insightful podcasts, make sure your content provides value to your audience. This will motivate them to sign up for your email list to receive more of it.

2. Opt-in incentives: To entice your audience to join your email list, offer them something valuable in return. This could be an exclusive ebook, a free course, or a discount code. Opt-in incentives are a great way to capture your audience's attention and encourage them to share their email addresses with you.

3. Optimize your sign-up forms: Place sign-up forms strategically on your website, blog, or YouTube channel. Make them visually appealing and easy to fill out. Consider using pop-ups, slide-ins, or embedded forms to capture your audience's attention.

4. Offer personalized content: Segment your email list based on your audience's interests and preferences. Send personalized content to each segment, ensuring that you are providing tailored information that resonates with them. This will make your subscribers feel valued and increase engagement.

5. Engage with your subscribers: Building an email list is not just about collecting email addresses; it's about building relationships. Ask for feedback, respond to queries, and engage with your subscribers regularly. This will foster a sense of community and loyalty among your audience.

Remember, building an email list takes time and effort. But the rewards are worth it. With a strong email list, you have a direct line of communication with your audience, allowing you to promote your content, products, and services effectively. So, start implementing these strategies and watch your email list grow, bringing you closer to your digital marketing goals.

Segmenting Your Subscribers for Targeted Campaigns

Segmenting Your Subscribers for Targeted Campaigns

In the ever-evolving world of digital marketing, one-size-fits-all campaigns are a thing of the past. As a content creator, digital creator, or social media influencer in the niche of digital marketing, it is essential to understand the importance of segmenting your subscribers for targeted campaigns. This subchapter will guide you through the process of effectively segmenting your subscriber base to maximize the impact of your marketing efforts.

Segmentation is the process of dividing your subscriber list into smaller, more specific groups based on certain criteria. By segmenting your subscribers, you can create customized campaigns that resonate with each group, resulting in higher engagement, conversion rates, and overall success.

The first step in segmenting your subscribers is to gather data. You can collect valuable information about your subscribers through sign-up forms, surveys, or by analyzing their behavior and preferences. This data will help you identify common characteristics, interests, and demographics among your subscribers, allowing you to create more targeted campaigns.

Once you have collected enough data, you can start creating segments based on specific criteria. These criteria can include demographics such as age, gender, location, or profession. Additionally, you can segment based on interests, purchasing behavior, engagement level, or even by the type of content they consume from your platform.

Segmenting your subscribers allows you to tailor your content and messaging to each group's preferences and needs. For example, if you have a segment of subscribers who are interested in email marketing, you can send them exclusive content, tips, and offers related to that topic. By doing so, you increase the chances of them engaging with your content and taking the desired action.

Furthermore, segmentation enables you to send targeted campaigns at the right time. By analyzing subscribers' behavior and engagement patterns, you can identify the best times to send emails or post content on social media platforms. This strategic approach ensures that your messages reach the right people at the right time, enhancing the effectiveness of your campaigns.

Segmenting your subscribers for targeted campaigns is a powerful strategy that can significantly impact your digital marketing efforts. By understanding your audience better and tailoring your content to their specific needs, you can foster stronger connections, build trust, and ultimately drive better results.

In the next subchapter, we will delve into the various tools and platforms available to help you segment your subscribers effectively, along with best practices for creating personalized and impactful campaigns. Stay tuned for more valuable insights on how to master digital marketing as a content creator, digital creator, or social media influencer in the niche of digital marketing.

Designing Effective Email Campaigns

Designing Effective Email Campaigns

Email marketing is a powerful tool for content creators, digital creators, and social media influencers to connect with their audience and promote their digital marketing efforts. In this subchapter, we will explore the key elements and strategies to design effective email campaigns that drive engagement, conversions, and ultimately, success.

1. Define Your Goals: Before diving into designing your email campaigns, it is crucial to define your goals. Are you aiming to increase website traffic, promote a new product or service, or simply nurture your audience? Having a clear goal in mind will help you shape your campaign and measure its success.

2. Understand Your Audience: To create effective email campaigns, you need to understand your audience's preferences, interests, and needs. Segment your email list based on demographics, purchase history, or engagement levels to personalize your content and deliver tailored messages that resonate with your subscribers.

3. Craft Compelling Subject Lines: The subject line is the first impression your email makes, so make it count. Grab your audience's attention with concise, compelling subject lines that entice them to open your emails. Use action words, personalization, and urgency to increase open rates.

4. Engaging Content: The content of your emails should be engaging, informative, and valuable to your subscribers. Share exclusive content, industry insights, tips, or special offers to keep your audience interested and eager to open future emails. Use a conversational tone and include visuals to make your emails more visually appealing.

5. Call-to-Action (CTA): A strong, clear call-to-action is vital to drive desired actions from your subscribers. Whether it's directing them to your website, encouraging them to make a purchase, or asking them to share your content, ensure your CTA stands out and is easily clickable.

6. Mobile-Friendly Design: With the majority of emails being opened on mobile devices, it is essential to design your emails with a mobile-first mindset. Optimize your email templates for mobile screens, use responsive design, and keep your content concise and easy to read.

7. Testing and Analytics: Testing different elements of your email campaigns, such as subject lines, CTAs, or visuals, can provide valuable insights into what resonates best with your audience. Use A/B testing and analyze the analytics to refine and improve your campaigns continuously.

8. Automation and Personalization: Utilize email automation tools to streamline your campaigns and send personalized messages based on subscriber behavior, such as abandoned cart reminders or personalized recommendations. Personalization increases engagement and fosters stronger connections with your audience.

By following these strategies and best practices, you can design effective email campaigns that not only reach your audience but also drive meaningful results in your digital marketing efforts. Remember, consistency, relevance, and value are key to building a strong email marketing strategy that helps you achieve your goals and strengthen your relationship with your audience.

Writing Engaging Email Copy

Writing Engaging Email Copy

In the world of digital marketing, email remains a powerful tool for connecting with your audience, driving traffic, and increasing conversions. However, with inboxes flooded with countless emails every day, it's essential to create engaging email copy that stands out from the crowd. This subchapter will provide valuable insights and strategies to help content creators, digital creators, and social media influencers master the art of writing compelling email copy.

1. Know Your Audience:
Before crafting any email, it's crucial to understand your target audience. Define their demographics, interests, pain points, and preferences. Tailor your email copy to resonate with their needs, desires, and aspirations. Personalization is key to capturing their attention and fostering a genuine connection.

2. Grab Attention with a Strong Subject Line:

The subject line is the first thing your audience sees in their inbox, and it determines whether they'll open your email or not. Use creative, attention-grabbing subject lines that pique curiosity, offer value, or evoke emotions. Experiment with different lengths, tone, and formats to discover what works best for your audience.

3. Craft Compelling Introduction:

The first few sentences of your email are crucial for hooking your readers. Use a conversational tone, ask intriguing questions, or share a fascinating story to captivate their interest. Make it clear why your email is worth their time and what they stand to gain from reading further.

4. Focus on Benefits, Not Features:

When promoting a product or service, don't simply list its features. Instead, highlight the benefits it can provide to your audience. Explain how it solves their problems, saves time, enhances their lives, or fulfills their desires. Use persuasive language and provide concrete examples to illustrate the value they'll receive.

5. Use Clear and Concise Language:

Avoid jargon, complicated language, or excessive fluff in your email copy. Keep your message clear, concise, and easy to understand. Use short paragraphs, bullet points, and subheadings to break up text and make it scannable. Remember, attention spans are short, so get to the point quickly.

6. Create a Sense of Urgency:

To encourage immediate action, create a sense of urgency in your email copy. Limited-time offers, exclusive discounts, or early-bird access can drive conversions. Use persuasive language to convey the urgency and emphasize the potential loss if they don't take action.

7. Include a Clear Call-to-Action (CTA):

Every email should have a clear and compelling call-to-action. Whether it's to visit a website, make a purchase, subscribe, or share content, guide your readers with a prominent and visually appealing CTA button. Use persuasive language to motivate action and provide a sense of urgency.

By implementing these strategies, content creators, digital creators, and social media influencers can write engaging email copy that grabs attention, connects with their audience, and drives desired actions. Remember to test and analyze your email campaigns to continually refine your approach and maximize results.

Utilizing Automation and Personalization

Utilizing Automation and Personalization

In the ever-evolving world of digital marketing, content creators, digital creators, and social media influencers need to stay ahead of the game. One way to do this is by harnessing the power of automation and personalization. These two key strategies can revolutionize your digital marketing efforts, allowing you to connect with your target audience on a deeper level and achieve even greater success.

Automation is all about streamlining your processes and saving valuable time. As a content creator, you understand the importance of consistency and delivering high-quality content to your audience. With automation tools, you can schedule your posts, automate email campaigns, and even manage your social media accounts more efficiently. This not only frees up your time but also ensures that your content is consistently being shared with your followers, enhancing your brand visibility and engagement.

Personalization, on the other hand, is all about tailoring your content to meet the unique needs and preferences of your audience. In the digital marketing sphere, personalization has become increasingly important as consumers crave a more personalized experience. By utilizing data analytics and customer insights, you can create targeted content that resonates with your audience, driving higher engagement and conversion rates. Personalization can be as simple as addressing your audience by their names in your email campaigns or as complex as creating personalized landing pages based on their browsing behavior.

It is worth noting that automation and personalization go hand in hand. By leveraging automation tools, you can gather valuable data and insights about your audience, which can then be used to personalize your content. For example, you can use automation to segment your email list based on interests or demographics and then send personalized content to each segment. This not only increases the relevance of your content but also builds trust and loyalty with your audience.

As a content creator, digital creator, or social media influencer, incorporating automation and personalization into your digital marketing strategy is crucial for success. By doing so, you can streamline your processes, deliver consistent and high-quality content, and connect with your audience on a deeper level. Embrace the power of automation and personalization, and watch your digital marketing efforts soar to new heights.

Chapter 5: Maximizing Video Marketing

Embracing the Rise of Video Content

Embracing the Rise of Video Content

In today's digital age, it is impossible to ignore the power and influence of video content. From YouTube to Instagram and TikTok, video has become the preferred medium for content consumption. As content creators, digital creators, and social media influencers, it is crucial to understand and embrace the rise of video content, as it presents a unique opportunity to engage with your audience and grow your online presence.

Video content offers numerous advantages over other forms of content. Firstly, it is highly engaging and captivating. With the ability to combine visuals, audio, and storytelling, videos have the power to evoke emotions, tell compelling narratives, and leave a lasting impact on viewers. This level of engagement is unmatched by any other content format, making video an ideal tool for digital marketing.

Additionally, video content has a higher potential for virality. Platforms like YouTube and TikTok have algorithms that prioritize video content, making it easier for your videos to reach a wider audience. By creating shareable and memorable videos, you can increase your chances of going viral and gaining substantial exposure for your brand or content.

Moreover, video content allows for greater creativity and versatility. Whether it's through tutorials, vlogs, interviews, or behind-the-scenes footage, videos provide endless opportunities to showcase your skills, expertise, and personality. By leveraging video content, you can establish a strong personal brand and connect with your audience on a deeper level.

To fully embrace the rise of video content, it is essential to optimize your digital marketing strategies accordingly. Start by identifying your target audience and understanding their preferences and interests. This will help you create video content that resonates with them and captures their attention.

Invest in quality equipment, such as cameras, lighting, and microphones, to ensure your videos are visually appealing and professionally produced. Additionally, focus on storytelling and creating narratives that evoke emotions and leave a lasting impact. Remember that authenticity is key, so be genuine and true to yourself in your videos.

Finally, leverage the power of social media platforms to distribute and promote your video content. Utilize hashtags, engage with your audience, and collaborate with other content creators to expand your reach and visibility.

In conclusion, embracing the rise of video content is pivotal for content creators, digital creators, and social media influencers in the digital marketing sphere. By understanding the advantages of video content, optimizing your strategies, and leveraging social media platforms, you can effectively engage with your audience, grow your online presence, and achieve your digital marketing goals.

Understanding the Benefits of Video Marketing

Understanding the Benefits of Video Marketing

In today's digital age, where content is king, video marketing has become a powerful tool for content creators, digital creators, and social media influencers. The ability to engage and captivate audiences through visual storytelling has made video marketing an essential component of any successful digital marketing strategy. In this subchapter, we will explore the numerous benefits that video marketing can offer in the realm of content creation and digital marketing.

First and foremost, video marketing has the ability to convey complex messages in a concise and compelling manner. Through the use of visuals, motion, and sound, content creators can effectively communicate their ideas, products, or services to their target audience. This not only boosts engagement but also enhances comprehension and retention of the message being delivered. Whether it's a tutorial, a product review, or a brand story, video marketing allows for a richer and more immersive experience for viewers.

Moreover, video marketing has proven to be highly shareable across various social media platforms. The human brain is naturally drawn to visual content, and videos have the potential to go viral, reaching a wider audience than any other form of content. With the ability to evoke emotions, entertain, and educate, videos have the power to create a strong emotional connection with viewers, leading to increased brand awareness and loyalty.

Additionally, video marketing can greatly improve search engine optimization (SEO) efforts. Search engines prioritize video content, and by incorporating relevant keywords, tags, and descriptions, content creators can increase their visibility in search engine results pages. This not only drives organic traffic to their websites but also improves their overall online presence.

Furthermore, video marketing offers a unique opportunity for content creators to showcase their personality, creativity, and authenticity. Viewers are more likely to connect with individuals who appear genuine and relatable, and video marketing allows content creators to establish a personal connection with their audience. By leveraging their expertise and unique voice, digital creators and social media influencers can build a loyal community of followers who trust and respect their recommendations.

In conclusion, video marketing has revolutionized the world of digital marketing for content creators, digital creators, and social media influencers. Its ability to engage, share, optimize, and create personal connections makes it an invaluable tool for anyone in the digital marketing niche. By harnessing the power of video marketing, content creators can take their digital presence to new heights and reach a wider audience than ever before.

Choosing the Right Video Platforms for Your Content

Choosing the Right Video Platforms for Your Content

In today's digital age, video has become one of the most powerful forms of content. As a content creator, digital creator, or social media influencer, it is essential to understand the importance of choosing the right video platforms to maximize your reach and engagement. This subchapter will guide you through the process of selecting the ideal video platforms for your content, allowing you to effectively showcase your work and connect with your target audience.

When determining the appropriate video platforms for your content, it is crucial to consider your niche, target audience, and marketing goals. Each platform has its unique features and user demographics, which can significantly impact your content's success. Here are a few popular video platforms to consider:

1. YouTube: As the largest video-sharing platform, YouTube offers a vast audience and various content opportunities. Ideal for long-form videos, tutorials, or educational content, YouTube allows you to build a dedicated subscriber base and monetize your videos through ads or sponsorships.

2. Instagram: Known for its visual content, Instagram is perfect for short and visually appealing videos. With features like IGTV and Stories, you can showcase behind-the-scenes footage, product reviews, or snippets of your content to capture your audience's attention.

3. TikTok: This rapidly growing platform is ideal for short, creative, and entertaining videos. TikTok's algorithm-driven content discovery can help your videos reach a wider audience, making it an excellent choice for content creators seeking to go viral or target a younger demographic.

4. Vimeo: If you are looking for a more professional and high-quality video platform, Vimeo is an excellent choice. Targeting a more niche audience, Vimeo allows for advanced customization, privacy control, and superior video quality, making it a preferred option for filmmakers and artists.

5. LinkedIn: For those in the digital marketing niche, LinkedIn can be a powerful platform to share industry-related videos, tutorials, or thought leadership content. With its professional focus, LinkedIn can help you establish yourself as an expert in your field and connect with potential clients or collaborators.

Remember that selecting the right video platforms is not a one-size-fits-all approach. It's essential to research and experiment with different platforms to find the ones that align with your content, target audience, and overall marketing strategy. By choosing the right video platforms, you can enhance your digital marketing efforts, expand your reach, and cultivate a loyal following of engaged viewers.

Creating Professional and Engaging Videos

Creating Professional and Engaging Videos

In today's digital landscape, video content has become a powerful tool for content creators, digital creators, and social media influencers to connect with their audience and drive engagement. With the ever-growing popularity of platforms like YouTube, Instagram, and TikTok, mastering the art of creating professional and engaging videos is crucial to succeed in the realm of digital marketing.

1. Planning Your Video: Before hitting the record button, it is essential to have a clear plan in mind. Determine your target audience, the purpose of your video, and the key message you want to convey. Outline a script or create a storyboard to ensure a well-structured video that engages your viewers from start to finish.

2. Quality Equipment: Invest in good quality equipment to ensure professional-looking videos. A high-resolution camera, a stable tripod, and a quality microphone can greatly enhance the production value of your videos. Remember, a visually appealing and crisp video with clear audio will captivate your audience and keep them coming back for more.

3. Lighting and Background: Pay attention to your lighting setup and background. Good lighting can make a significant difference in the overall quality of your video. Natural light is ideal, but if that's not possible, invest in affordable lighting kits to achieve a well-lit video. Additionally, choose a background that is visually appealing and relevant to your content. A clutter-free and well-organized background will keep the focus on you and your message.

4. Engaging Content: Create content that resonates with your audience. Develop a unique style that reflects your personality and brand. Keep your videos informative, entertaining, and relevant to your niche. Incorporate storytelling techniques, visuals, and graphics to make your videos visually appealing and engaging.

5. Editing and Post-production: Editing is a crucial step in creating professional videos. Utilize video editing software to trim unnecessary footage, add transitions, overlays, and effects, and enhance the overall quality of your video. Pay attention to the pacing, audio levels, and color correction to create a polished final product.

6. Optimizing for SEO: To maximize the reach and visibility of your videos, optimize them for search engines. Use relevant keywords in your video titles, descriptions, and tags. This will help your videos rank higher in search results, making it easier for your target audience to find you.

Creating professional and engaging videos is a skill that can greatly impact your success as a content creator, digital creator, or social media influencer. By following these tips and continuously honing your craft, you can unlock the true potential of video marketing and build a loyal and engaged audience in the world of digital marketing.

Video Production Techniques for Content Creators

Video Production Techniques for Content Creators

In this subchapter, we will explore essential video production techniques specifically tailored for content creators in the digital marketing niche. As a content creator, digital creator, or social media influencer, incorporating videos into your content strategy can greatly enhance your reach and engagement with your audience. By understanding and implementing these video production techniques, you will be able to create compelling and professional-looking videos that captivate your viewers and drive your digital marketing efforts to new heights.

1. Planning and Storyboarding: Before diving into production, it is crucial to plan your video content meticulously. Create a storyboard outlining the flow, shots, and narrative of your video. This will ensure a coherent and well-structured video that effectively conveys your message.

2. Lighting and Framing: Proper lighting and framing can significantly impact the quality of your videos. Invest in good lighting equipment or utilize natural lighting to create a visually appealing atmosphere. Experiment with different framing techniques to add depth and visual interest to your shots.

3. Audio Quality: High-quality audio is equally important as video quality. Invest in a good microphone to ensure clear and crisp sound. Minimize background noise and consider adding background music or voiceovers to enhance the overall audio experience.

4. Editing and Post-production: The editing process is where your video truly comes to life. Utilize professional video editing software to fine-tune your footage, add special effects, transitions, and overlays. Pay attention to color grading to create a cohesive and visually appealing look.

5. Captions and Subtitles: Including captions and subtitles in your videos can make them more accessible to a wider audience. It enables viewers to understand your content even in noisy or quiet environments and improves search engine optimization.

6. Engaging Thumbnails and Titles: To attract viewers, your video's thumbnail and title should be eye-catching and enticing. Craft engaging titles and create customized thumbnails that accurately represent the content and evoke curiosity.

7. Consistency and Branding: Maintain a consistent visual style and branding across your video content. This will help your audience recognize and connect with your brand more easily, enhancing brand loyalty and recognition.

By implementing these video production techniques, content creators, digital creators, and social media influencers in the digital marketing niche can create compelling videos that engage and resonate with their audience. Remember to always experiment, learn from feedback, and continuously improve your video production skills to stay ahead in the ever-evolving digital marketing landscape.

Incorporating Storytelling into Your Videos

Incorporating Storytelling into Your Videos

In the fast-paced world of digital marketing, content creators, digital creators, and social media influencers are constantly seeking new ways to engage their audience and stand out from the crowd. One powerful technique that has proven to be effective time and time again is incorporating storytelling into your videos.

Storytelling has a unique ability to captivate an audience and evoke emotions. By integrating storytelling into your videos, you can create a deeper connection with your viewers and leave a lasting impression. Here are some tips on how to incorporate storytelling into your video content:

1. Begin with a compelling narrative: Every great story starts with a compelling beginning. Hook your viewers from the start by introducing a captivating narrative that sparks curiosity and keeps them engaged throughout the video.

2. Develop relatable characters: Characters play a crucial role in storytelling. Create relatable characters that your audience can connect with. This will help them feel emotionally invested in your video and keep them coming back for more.

3. Use visual storytelling techniques: Don't just rely on dialogue to tell your story. Utilize visual storytelling techniques such as cinematography, editing, and music to enhance the emotional impact of your videos. Every shot, transition, and piece of music should contribute to the overall narrative.

4. Incorporate real-life examples: Real-life examples and case studies can add credibility to your storytelling. By showcasing real people and their experiences, you can make your content more relatable and authentic.

5. Create a story arc: Just like in movies or books, your video content should follow a story arc. Start with an introduction, build up the conflict or problem, provide a resolution, and end with a memorable conclusion. This will keep your viewers engaged and satisfied.

6. Be consistent with your brand: While storytelling is crucial, don't forget to align your videos with your brand's identity. Maintain consistency in terms of tone, style, and messaging to ensure your storytelling efforts support your overall digital marketing strategy.

Incorporating storytelling into your videos can transform your content from ordinary to extraordinary. It allows you to connect with your audience on a deeper level, build brand loyalty, and drive engagement. So, whether you're a content creator, digital creator, or social media influencer, harness the power of storytelling and watch your videos come to life.

Chapter 6: Analyzing and Optimizing Your Digital Marketing Efforts

Tracking Key Performance Indicators (KPIs)

Tracking Key Performance Indicators (KPIs)

In today's digital landscape, understanding and tracking key performance indicators (KPIs) is crucial for content creators, digital creators, and social media influencers looking to excel in the field of digital marketing. KPIs serve as measurable metrics that provide valuable insights into the success of your content and overall digital marketing efforts. By effectively tracking these KPIs, you can optimize your strategies, identify areas of improvement, and drive better results.

One of the most important KPIs to track is website traffic. This metric allows you to monitor the number of visitors to your website, where they come from, and which pages they engage with the most. By leveraging tools like Google Analytics, you can gain a comprehensive understanding of your audience's behavior and preferences, enabling you to create more targeted and effective content.

Another vital KPI is conversion rate, which measures the percentage of website visitors who take a desired action, such as making a purchase, subscribing to a newsletter, or filling out a form. A high conversion rate signifies that your content is compelling and resonates with your audience, while a low conversion rate may indicate a need for improvement or optimization in your marketing strategies.

Engagement metrics, including likes, shares, comments, and followers, are crucial for content creators and social media influencers. These metrics reflect the level of engagement and interaction your content generates. Tracking these KPIs allows you to gauge the impact and reach of your digital marketing efforts, helping you understand what resonates with your audience and what doesn't.

Furthermore, tracking KPIs related to social media reach and engagement can provide valuable insights into the effectiveness of your social media marketing campaigns. Metrics such as reach, impressions, click-through rates, and engagement rates allow you to measure the success of your social media content, identify trends, and optimize your strategies accordingly.

Lastly, tracking KPIs related to customer satisfaction and feedback is crucial for content creators and digital marketers. By leveraging tools like surveys, customer reviews, and testimonials, you can gather valuable insights into your audience's satisfaction and preferences. This information can help you refine your content, identify new opportunities, and build stronger relationships with your audience.

In conclusion, tracking key performance indicators (KPIs) is essential for content creators, digital creators, and social media influencers in the field of digital marketing. By monitoring metrics such as website traffic, conversion rates, engagement, social media reach, and customer satisfaction, you can gain valuable insights into the success of your digital marketing strategies. Armed with this information, you can optimize your content, refine your marketing campaigns, and achieve greater success in the ever-evolving world of digital marketing.

Identifying Relevant Metrics for Content Creators

Identifying Relevant Metrics for Content Creators

In the fast-paced world of digital marketing, content creators have become the driving force behind successful campaigns. Whether you are a blogger, vlogger, social media influencer, or any other type of digital creator, understanding the metrics that matter is crucial for your success. Tracking and analyzing relevant metrics not only helps you measure the effectiveness of your content but also provides valuable insights for future strategies.

When it comes to identifying relevant metrics, content creators should focus on those that align with their goals and objectives. While there are numerous metrics available, it's essential to choose the ones that make the most sense for your niche and digital marketing efforts.

One of the primary metrics to consider is audience engagement. This includes likes, comments, shares, and any other form of interaction your audience has with your content. High engagement rates indicate that your content is resonating with your target audience, driving conversations, and fostering a sense of community around your brand.

Another crucial metric is reach, which measures the number of unique users who have seen your content. A higher reach means that your content is being exposed to a wider audience, potentially increasing brand awareness and attracting new followers.

For content creators who monetize their platforms through advertising or sponsorships, metrics such as impressions and click-through rates (CTRs) are essential. Impressions measure the number of times your content is displayed, while CTRs indicate the percentage of viewers who click on a specific link. These metrics demonstrate the effectiveness of your content in generating interest and driving traffic to external websites.

Furthermore, conversion metrics are crucial for content creators who aim to drive specific actions from their audience, such as signing up for a newsletter or making a purchase. Conversion rate, cost per conversion, and return on investment (ROI) are valuable metrics to evaluate the effectiveness of your content in achieving these goals.

Lastly, content creators should not overlook metrics related to audience demographics and behavior. Understanding your audience's age, gender, location, and interests allows you to tailor your content to their preferences, ensuring higher engagement rates and overall success.

In conclusion, identifying relevant metrics is a fundamental step for content creators in the digital marketing space. By focusing on metrics that align with their goals and objectives, content creators can measure the effectiveness of their content, make data-driven decisions, and continuously improve their strategies. Remember, tracking and analyzing metrics isn't just about numbers—it's about understanding your audience, optimizing your content, and ultimately achieving success in the competitive world of digital marketing.

Utilizing Analytics Tools to Measure Success

Utilizing Analytics Tools to Measure Success

In the ever-evolving world of digital marketing, content creators, digital creators, and social media influencers must stay at the forefront of their game to drive success. One key aspect of achieving this success is understanding the power of analytics tools and how they can be used to measure the effectiveness of your strategies. In this subchapter, we will dive into the importance of analytics tools and how they can help you elevate your digital marketing game.

Analytics tools provide invaluable insights into the performance of your content and campaigns. They allow you to track key metrics such as website traffic, engagement rates, click-through rates, conversion rates, and more. By analyzing this data, you can identify trends, understand your audience's behavior, and make data-driven decisions to optimize your marketing efforts.

One of the most popular analytics tools for content creators and digital marketers is Google Analytics. This powerful tool offers a comprehensive view of your website's performance, providing crucial data such as the number of visitors, their demographics, the sources of traffic, and the pages they engage with the most. Armed with this information, you can refine your content strategy, tailor your messaging, and target your audience more effectively.

Social media platforms also provide their own analytics tools. Facebook Insights, Instagram Insights, and Twitter Analytics, for example, offer detailed data on post reach, engagement, and follower demographics. By studying these analytics, you can determine which types of content resonate best with your audience and optimize your social media strategy accordingly.

In addition to these platform-specific tools, there are also third-party analytics tools available that can further enhance your measurement capabilities. Tools like Hootsuite, Sprout Social, and Buffer provide in-depth social media analytics, allowing you to track your performance across multiple platforms, schedule posts, and generate reports to assess your success.

Remember, analytics tools are only valuable if you use them effectively. Regularly monitoring and analyzing your data is crucial for understanding what works and what doesn't. By identifying your top-performing content, you can replicate its success, while also learning from underperforming posts to make improvements.

In conclusion, analytics tools are a game-changer for content creators, digital creators, and social media influencers in the field of digital marketing. These tools provide valuable insights into the performance of your content and campaigns, allowing you to optimize your strategies and drive success. By leveraging tools like Google Analytics, social media platform insights, and third-party analytics tools, you can gain a deep understanding of your audience, tailor your content, and ultimately achieve your digital marketing goals.

A/B Testing and Conversion Rate Optimization

A/B Testing and Conversion Rate Optimization

In the fast-paced world of digital marketing, staying ahead of the competition is crucial for content creators, digital creators, and social media influencers. To achieve success, it is essential to understand the concepts of A/B testing and conversion rate optimization. These strategies can significantly improve your digital marketing efforts and help you achieve higher engagement and conversion rates.

A/B testing is a method used to compare two versions of a webpage or marketing campaign to determine which one performs better. By creating two variations, A and B, and then splitting your audience into two groups, you can analyze the effectiveness of different elements such as headlines, images, call-to-actions, or even entire landing pages. This data-driven approach allows you to make informed decisions based on real user behavior, enabling you to optimize your content for maximum impact.

Conversion rate optimization (CRO) is the process of increasing the percentage of website visitors who take a desired action, such as making a purchase, signing up for a newsletter, or filling out a contact form. By constantly analyzing the data from A/B tests and implementing changes accordingly, you can optimize your website or marketing campaign to convert more visitors into customers or followers.

For content creators, A/B testing and CRO can be game-changers. You can experiment with different types of content, headlines, or visuals to determine what resonates best with your audience. By optimizing your content, you can increase user engagement, time spent on your website, and ultimately, conversions.

For digital creators and social media influencers, A/B testing can be applied to your social media posts, email marketing campaigns, or even video content. By testing different variations of your content, you can identify what type of content your audience prefers, leading to higher engagement rates, more followers, and increased brand loyalty.

In the world of digital marketing, data is power. A/B testing and conversion rate optimization allow you to make data-driven decisions rather than relying on guesswork or assumptions. By continuously testing and optimizing your content, you can stay ahead of the competition, attract more followers, and achieve your digital marketing goals.

In conclusion, A/B testing and conversion rate optimization are essential strategies for content creators, digital creators, and social media influencers in the field of digital marketing. By implementing these strategies, you can harness the power of data to optimize your content for higher engagement, conversions, and ultimately, success in the digital realm.

Experimenting with Different Strategies

Experimenting with Different Strategies

As content creators, digital creators, and social media influencers, it's essential to constantly evolve and adapt your digital marketing strategies. In the ever-changing landscape of digital marketing, staying ahead of the curve is crucial for success. This subchapter will delve into the significance of experimenting with different strategies to optimize your digital marketing efforts and achieve your goals.

The world of digital marketing is diverse and multifaceted, offering countless opportunities for growth and engagement. However, what works for one content creator may not necessarily yield the same results for another. This is why experimenting with different strategies is vital. By testing various tactics, you can identify what resonates best with your audience, allowing you to refine your approach and maximize your impact.

One effective strategy to experiment with is content format. Consider exploring different types of content, such as blog posts, videos, podcasts, or infographics, to determine which format garners the most engagement from your audience. Analyze metrics such as views, likes, shares, and comments to gain insights into what captivates your viewers and generates the most interest.

Furthermore, experimenting with platforms can significantly amplify your digital marketing efforts. While social media platforms like Instagram and YouTube are popular among content creators, it's important to keep an eye on emerging platforms, such as TikTok or Clubhouse. Testing these newer platforms can help you reach a wider audience and tap into new communities that align with your niche.

Additionally, don't shy away from trying different marketing techniques. Whether it's influencer collaborations, email marketing campaigns, or search engine optimization (SEO) strategies, experimenting with these tactics can provide valuable insights into what drives traffic, increases engagement, and boosts conversions.

Remember, experimentation requires a structured approach. Set clear objectives for each experiment, establish a timeframe, and track your progress meticulously. Analyzing the results will enable you to make data-driven decisions and refine your strategies accordingly.

In conclusion, as content creators, digital creators, and social media influencers, it's crucial to embrace experimentation as a core component of your digital marketing journey. By testing different strategies, formats, platforms, and marketing techniques, you'll gain invaluable insights into what resonates with your audience and how you can optimize your efforts. Embrace the ever-changing digital marketing landscape, and let experimentation be your guide to success.

Improving Website Conversion Rates

Improving Website Conversion Rates

In the fast-paced world of digital marketing, maximizing your website's conversion rates is crucial for success. As content creators, digital creators, and social media influencers, your online presence is your key to reaching a wider audience and driving engagement. This subchapter will delve into effective strategies and techniques to enhance your website's conversion rates, ensuring that your efforts translate into tangible results in the realm of digital marketing.

One of the first steps in improving website conversion rates is understanding your target audience. By identifying their needs, preferences, and pain points, you can tailor your content to resonate with them. Conduct thorough market research and leverage analytics tools to gain insights into your audience's demographics, interests, and browsing behavior. Armed with this knowledge, you can create compelling content that speaks directly to your target audience, increasing the likelihood of conversions.

Optimizing your website's user experience (UX) is another critical aspect of improving conversion rates. Ensure that your website is visually appealing, easy to navigate, and mobile-friendly. A seamless and intuitive user interface will encourage visitors to explore your content further and take desired actions, such as subscribing to newsletters or making purchases. Implement clear call-to-action buttons strategically throughout your website, guiding users towards conversion points and simplifying the conversion process.

Another effective strategy is to leverage social proof. As influential content creators, you have the advantage of a loyal following. Encourage your audience to leave testimonials, reviews, or share their success stories related to your products or services. Displaying these positive affirmations on your website builds trust and credibility, convincing potential customers to convert. Additionally, consider incorporating social media feeds or follower counts to highlight your popularity and engage visitors.

To optimize conversion rates, it's essential to continuously test and refine your strategies. Utilize A/B testing to compare different versions of landing pages, headlines, or calls-to-action. Analyze the results to determine which elements perform best and make data-driven decisions accordingly. Regularly monitor your website's performance through analytics tools, identifying areas for improvement and implementing necessary changes.

In conclusion, improving website conversion rates is a vital aspect of digital marketing for content creators, digital creators, and social media influencers. By understanding your target audience, optimizing UX, leveraging social proof, and continuously testing and refining your strategies, you can enhance your website's performance and achieve higher conversion rates. These efforts will help you expand your reach, increase engagement, and ultimately drive success in the ever-evolving world of digital marketing.

Chapter 7: Staying Ahead in the Digital Marketing Landscape

Keeping Up with Emerging Digital Marketing Trends

Keeping Up with Emerging Digital Marketing Trends

In the fast-paced world of digital marketing, staying ahead of the game is crucial for content creators, digital creators, and social media influencers. The landscape of digital marketing is constantly evolving, with new trends and technologies emerging regularly. To succeed in this ever-changing environment, it is essential to keep up with the latest trends and adapt your strategies accordingly.

One of the most important aspects of staying updated with emerging digital marketing trends is understanding your audience. By knowing your target audience's preferences and behaviors, you can tailor your content and marketing strategies to meet their needs. Conducting regular market research and analysis will help you identify emerging trends and adapt your content creation accordingly.

Video marketing has become an integral part of digital marketing, with platforms like YouTube and TikTok dominating the online space. As a content creator or digital creator, incorporating video content into your marketing strategy is essential to engage and captivate your audience. Whether it's creating tutorials, behind-the-scenes content, or vlogs, video content allows you to connect with your audience on a more personal and authentic level.

Another emerging trend in digital marketing is influencer collaborations. Social media influencers have gained significant influence over their followers, and partnering with them can help expand your reach and build credibility. Collaborating with influencers in your niche can help you tap into their established audience and create authentic content that resonates with their followers.

Furthermore, keeping up with the latest social media trends is crucial for digital marketers. Platforms like Instagram, Facebook, and Twitter are constantly updating their algorithms and introducing new features. It is essential to familiarize yourself with these changes and adapt your content creation and marketing strategies accordingly. Whether it's utilizing Instagram Reels, creating interactive Facebook content, or leveraging Twitter Spaces, staying up-to-date with social media trends will help you stay ahead of the competition.

In addition to social media, emerging technologies like virtual reality (VR) and augmented reality (AR) are transforming the digital marketing landscape. These technologies offer unique opportunities for content creators to create immersive and interactive experiences for their audience. Exploring the possibilities of VR and AR can help you stand out from the crowd and provide your audience with memorable experiences.

To conclude, as a content creator, digital creator, or social media influencer, keeping up with emerging digital marketing trends is essential. By understanding your audience, incorporating video marketing, leveraging influencer collaborations, staying updated with social media trends, and exploring emerging technologies, you can stay ahead of the curve and achieve success in the ever-evolving field of digital marketing.

AI and Automation in Digital Marketing

AI and Automation in Digital Marketing

In today's digital age, AI (Artificial Intelligence) and automation have revolutionized the way businesses approach digital marketing. As content creators, digital creators, and social media influencers, it is crucial to understand the role AI and automation play in the realm of digital marketing. This subchapter aims to delve into the various ways AI and automation can enhance your digital marketing strategies, ultimately helping you to achieve your goals in this ever-evolving field.

First and foremost, AI brings a myriad of opportunities for content creators, digital creators, and social media influencers. With AI-powered algorithms, you can analyze vast amounts of data to gain valuable insights into consumer behavior, preferences, and trends. This data-driven approach allows you to create highly targeted and personalized content that resonates with your audience, leading to increased engagement and conversions.

Automation, on the other hand, streamlines and simplifies various aspects of digital marketing. For instance, AI-powered chatbots can handle customer inquiries, providing immediate responses and enhancing user experience. Additionally, automation tools can schedule and publish your content across multiple platforms, saving you time and effort while ensuring consistent delivery of your message.

Furthermore, AI and automation enable content creators to optimize their SEO strategies. AI algorithms can analyze search patterns and competition, helping you identify the most effective keywords and optimize your website's SEO accordingly. This ensures that your content ranks higher in search engine results, increasing your visibility and driving organic traffic to your website.

Moreover, AI and automation play a significant role in social media marketing. AI algorithms can analyze social media trends, helping you identify the best times to post, the most engaging content formats, and the most effective influencers to collaborate with. Automation tools can also help you schedule and manage your social media posts, ensuring a consistent presence across platforms and maximizing your reach.

However, it is important to note that while AI and automation offer numerous benefits, they should not replace human creativity and intuition. As content creators, digital creators, and social media influencers, your unique voice and perspective are what sets you apart. AI and automation should be seen as tools to enhance and optimize your digital marketing efforts, rather than replace the human touch.

In conclusion, AI and automation have become invaluable assets in the world of digital marketing. By leveraging AI algorithms and automation tools, content creators, digital creators, and social media influencers can gain deeper insights into their audience, streamline their processes, optimize their SEO strategies, and maximize their social media presence. Embracing AI and automation can significantly boost your digital marketing efforts, helping you thrive in the competitive landscape of content creation and digital influence.

Influencer Marketing and Collaborations

Influencer Marketing and Collaborations

In today's digital age, influencer marketing has emerged as a powerful tool for content creators, digital creators, and social media influencers to expand their reach, connect with their target audience, and monetize their content. This subchapter aims to provide a comprehensive guide to influencer marketing and collaborations, equipping content creators with the knowledge and strategies needed to thrive in the fast-paced world of digital marketing.

Understanding the Basics of Influencer Marketing
Influencer marketing involves partnering with influential individuals in your niche to promote your brand, product, or service. These influencers have built a loyal following and possess the ability to sway their audience's opinions and behaviors. By leveraging their influence, content creators can tap into a ready-made audience, resulting in increased brand visibility, credibility, and engagement.

Identifying the Right Influencers

The key to successful influencer marketing lies in finding the right influencer for your niche. In this subchapter, we will explore effective strategies to identify and evaluate potential influencers, considering factors such as audience demographics, engagement rates, brand alignment, and authenticity.

Crafting Effective Collaboration Strategies

Once you have identified the ideal influencers, it's crucial to develop a collaboration strategy that aligns with your goals. We will delve into various collaboration types, such as sponsored content, product reviews, brand ambassadorships, and affiliate partnerships, providing insights into best practices, negotiation techniques, and legal considerations.

Measuring Success and ROI

To determine the effectiveness of your influencer marketing campaigns, understanding how to measure success and calculate return on investment (ROI) is essential. We will discuss key performance indicators (KPIs) to track, tools for monitoring and analyzing data, and methods for assessing the impact of influencer collaborations on your brand.

Navigating Ethical and Legal Considerations

As influencer marketing continues to evolve, ethical and legal considerations have become increasingly important. This subchapter will address the Federal Trade Commission (FTC) guidelines, disclosure requirements, transparency, and authenticity, ensuring content creators understand how to maintain trust and compliance within the digital marketing landscape.

Building Long-Term Relationships

Lastly, we will explore the benefits of fostering long-term relationships with influencers. By nurturing these connections, content creators can establish mutually beneficial partnerships, tap into new opportunities, and create a network of trusted influencers for future collaborations.

Influencer marketing and collaborations have the potential to propel content creators, digital creators, and social media influencers to new heights in the digital marketing realm. This subchapter aims to equip you with the knowledge and strategies needed to harness the power of influencer marketing, allowing you to engage with your target audience, amplify your brand, and achieve long-term success in the world of digital marketing.

Networking and Collaborating with Industry Professionals

Networking and Collaborating with Industry Professionals

In the ever-evolving world of digital marketing, one of the most valuable assets you can have as a content creator is a strong network of industry professionals. Networking and collaborating with like-minded individuals not only opens doors to new opportunities but also helps you stay up-to-date with the latest trends and techniques in the field. In this subchapter, we will explore the importance of networking and collaborating with industry professionals and provide you with practical tips on how to build and maintain these valuable relationships.

Why is networking and collaborating important in digital marketing?

Networking and collaborating with industry professionals can offer numerous benefits for content creators, digital creators, and social media influencers in the field of digital marketing. Firstly, it provides you with the opportunity to learn from experienced individuals who have already achieved success in your niche. By engaging in conversations and sharing ideas, you can gain valuable insights that can help you refine your own strategies and improve your content.

Secondly, networking and collaborating can lead to exciting collaborations and partnerships. By teaming up with other content creators, you can create powerful, cross-promotional campaigns that expose your work to a wider audience. Collaborating with industry professionals also adds credibility to your brand, as it demonstrates that you are recognized and respected within your field.

Building and maintaining professional relationships

To build a strong network of industry professionals, start by attending industry events and conferences. These gatherings provide a platform for meeting like-minded individuals and creating meaningful connections. Be sure to introduce yourself, exchange business cards, and follow up with a personalized email or social media message after the event to nurture the relationship.

Another effective way to network is through online communities and social media platforms. Join relevant groups and engage in discussions to establish yourself as an active member of the community. Share valuable insights and offer support to others, as this will help you build credibility and attract the attention of potential collaborators.

Remember that networking is a two-way street. Be proactive in helping others achieve their goals, and they will be more likely to reciprocate. Look for opportunities to collaborate on projects, share each other's content, or even co-create valuable resources for your audience. By fostering a spirit of collaboration, you can create a network of industry professionals who are eager to support and promote your work.

In conclusion, networking and collaborating with industry professionals is essential for content creators, digital creators, and social media influencers in the field of digital marketing. By building and maintaining strong relationships, you can learn from experienced professionals, create exciting collaborations, and expand your reach. Embrace the power of networking and collaboration, and watch your digital marketing efforts soar to new heights.

Building Strategic Partnerships

Building Strategic Partnerships

In today's competitive digital landscape, content creators, digital creators, and social media influencers need to go beyond creating compelling content to capture the attention of their target audience. To truly succeed in the realm of digital marketing, it is essential to build strategic partnerships that can help amplify your brand, expand your reach, and drive meaningful engagement. In this subchapter, we will explore the significance of building strategic partnerships and provide actionable insights for content creators in the niche of digital marketing.

Strategic partnerships are collaborations between two or more entities that share a common goal or target audience. By joining forces with like-minded brands, influencers, or businesses, content creators can tap into new networks, leverage existing audiences, and enhance their overall digital marketing efforts.

One of the key benefits of strategic partnerships is the ability to reach a wider audience. By partnering with complementary brands or influencers, content creators can tap into their partner's existing audience, exposing their content to a new set of potential followers. This mutually beneficial relationship enables both parties to gain exposure, increase brand awareness, and ultimately drive more traffic to their respective platforms.

Furthermore, strategic partnerships can also open doors to new opportunities for collaboration and cross-promotion. By working together, content creators can create joint campaigns, collaborations, or even co-create content that resonates with both their audiences. This collaborative approach not only enhances the quality of content but also allows creators to tap into each other's expertise, leading to a more diverse and engaging experience for their audience.

To build successful strategic partnerships, content creators must first identify potential partners whose values align with their brand and niche. Research and reach out to influencers, brands, or businesses that share similar target audiences or have complementary offerings. It is crucial to establish a genuine connection and understand how your collaboration can benefit both parties involved.

Once a partnership is established, content creators should focus on nurturing and maintaining the relationship. Regular communication, reciprocation, and providing value to each other are key to building long-lasting partnerships. By continuously supporting and promoting each other's content, creators can create a strong bond that fosters growth and mutual success.

In conclusion, building strategic partnerships is an essential aspect of digital marketing for content creators. These collaborations offer the opportunity to expand reach, tap into new audiences, and create innovative content that resonates with a broader base. By identifying the right partners, nurturing relationships, and collaborating effectively, content creators in the niche of digital marketing can leverage strategic partnerships to unlock their full potential and achieve greater success in their digital marketing endeavors.

Leveraging the Power of Online Communities

Leveraging the Power of Online Communities

In today's digital age, the power of online communities has become undeniable. As content creators, digital creators, and social media influencers, you have a unique opportunity to tap into these communities and harness their potential to amplify your reach and impact. This subchapter will explore the various ways you can leverage the power of online communities to supercharge your digital marketing efforts and achieve unparalleled success.

First and foremost, understanding the dynamics of online communities is essential. These communities are formed around shared interests, passions, or goals, and they can be found across various platforms such as forums, social media groups, and niche-specific websites. Recognizing the value of these communities and actively participating in them enables you to connect with like-minded individuals who are genuinely interested in your content.

One of the most effective ways to leverage online communities is by engaging in conversations and providing valuable insights. By actively participating in discussions, answering questions, and offering expert advice, you position yourself as an authority in your niche. This not only helps you build credibility but also creates opportunities for collaboration and networking with other influencers and content creators.

Another powerful way to leverage online communities is by cross-promotion. Collaborating with other creators who have a similar target audience but offer complementary content can significantly expand your reach. By sharing each other's content, you tap into their community and expose your brand to a whole new set of potential followers and customers.

Additionally, creating your own online community can be a game-changer. Whether it's a private Facebook group, a forum, or a membership site, having a dedicated space for your most engaged audience allows you to foster deeper connections, offer exclusive content, and gather valuable feedback. This not only helps you build a loyal fan base but also enables you to gather insights that can shape your content strategy.

Furthermore, leveraging the power of user-generated content within online communities can amplify your brand's reach. Encouraging your audience to create and share their own content related to your brand or products not only boosts engagement but also acts as social proof, showcasing the authenticity and value of your brand to a wider audience.

In conclusion, the power of online communities cannot be underestimated in the world of digital marketing. By actively engaging, collaborating, and creating your own community, you can tap into a vast pool of like-minded individuals who are eager to connect, learn, and support each other. Embracing this power will undoubtedly elevate your content creation and digital marketing efforts to new heights of success.

Chapter 8: Legal Considerations for Content Creators

Understanding Copyright and Intellectual Property

Understanding Copyright and Intellectual Property

In today's digital age, content creators, digital creators, and social media influencers have become powerful forces in the world of digital marketing. They possess the ability to reach millions of people through their captivating content, and their influence can shape trends, opinions, and even consumer behavior. However, with great power comes great responsibility – and it is crucial for content creators to understand the complex landscape of copyright and intellectual property.

Copyright is a legal concept that grants exclusive rights to creators and owners of original works, such as music, photographs, videos, literature, and artwork. These rights protect the creators' ability to control and monetize their creations, preventing others from using or reproducing their work without permission. Understanding copyright is essential for content creators as it helps them avoid legal disputes, protects their own work, and ensures they respect the rights of others.

When it comes to digital marketing, the lines can sometimes blur between inspiration and infringement. It is important for content creators to be aware of the laws and regulations surrounding intellectual property, including copyright, trademarks, and patents. By respecting these rights, content creators can maintain their credibility and avoid potential legal consequences.

One of the key aspects of copyright is fair use, which allows limited use of copyrighted material without permission from the copyright owner. Fair use typically applies to purposes such as criticism, commentary, news reporting, teaching, and research. However, determining fair use can be subjective and should be approached with caution. It is advisable for content creators to seek legal advice if they are unsure about using copyrighted material.

To protect their own work, content creators should consider copyright registration. While copyright protection is automatic upon creation, registering the copyright provides additional legal benefits, such as the ability to sue for copyright infringement. Content creators should also consider using watermarks, metadata, or digital rights management tools to deter unauthorized use of their work.

In the world of digital marketing, intellectual property extends beyond copyrights. Trademarks protect brand names, logos, and slogans, while patents protect inventions and innovative processes. Content creators should be aware of these forms of intellectual property and take steps to avoid infringing upon them.

Understanding copyright and intellectual property is essential for content creators, digital creators, and social media influencers in the field of digital marketing. By respecting the rights of others, protecting their own work, and staying informed about the legal landscape, content creators can thrive in their respective niches while maintaining their integrity and avoiding legal complications.

Protecting Your Original Content

Subchapter: Protecting Your Original Content

In the fast-paced and ever-evolving world of digital marketing, content creators, digital creators, and social media influencers play a vital role in engaging audiences and driving brand success. As a content creator, it's crucial to not only focus on creating compelling and valuable content but also to protect your original work from unauthorized use or infringement. In this subchapter, we will explore effective strategies and tools to safeguard your intellectual property and ensure that your hard work remains protected.

1. Understanding Intellectual Property Rights:
Before diving into the practical steps to protect your content, it's essential to understand the concept of intellectual property rights. Intellectual property refers to creations of the mind, such as inventions, designs, logos, music, and written works, which are protected by copyright, trademark, or patent laws. Familiarize yourself with these laws and how they apply to your content to assert your rights and take appropriate action in case of infringement.

2. Copyright Protection:

Copyright is an automatic right that protects original creative works, including articles, photos, videos, and graphic designs. To protect your content, consider adding a copyright notice to your website or social media profiles, which will inform others about your ownership and deter potential infringers. Additionally, consider registering your copyright with the relevant authorities to strengthen your legal position and gain additional protection.

3. Watermarking and Metadata:

Watermarking your images or videos is an effective way to prevent unauthorized use or distribution. Embedding your logo or name onto your visual content ensures that even if it is shared or reposted, your ownership remains intact. Similarly, adding metadata to your files, such as copyright information, contact details, and usage terms, can deter potential infringers and help identify the original creator.

4. Monitoring and Enforcement:

Regularly monitor the web for any unauthorized use of your content. Utilize online tools and services that can scan the internet for copies or unauthorized sharing of your work. If you come across any infringement, promptly take action by sending cease and desist notices, filing DMCA takedown requests, or seeking legal assistance if required. Vigilance and swift action are key to protecting your content and preserving your rights.

5. Collaborate with Influencers and Brands:

When collaborating with other content creators or brands, ensure that clear agreements are in place to define the ownership and usage rights of the created content. Include clauses that protect your intellectual property and clearly state the permitted uses, duration, and any compensation involved. Open communication and proper contracts will help avoid potential disputes and protect your original content.

Remember, protecting your original content is not just about securing your rights; it also helps maintain your credibility and reputation as a content creator. By implementing these strategies and staying informed about changes in intellectual property laws, you can confidently navigate the digital marketing landscape and ensure that your hard work is respected and valued.

Avoiding Copyright Infringement

Avoiding Copyright Infringement

As a content creator, digital creator, or social media influencer operating in the realm of digital marketing, it is vital to understand and respect copyright laws and regulations. Failing to do so can result in serious legal consequences and damage to your online reputation. In this subchapter, we will explore the importance of avoiding copyright infringement and provide you with essential guidelines to navigate this complex terrain.

Copyright infringement occurs when someone uses, reproduces, or distributes copyrighted material without obtaining proper permission from the original creator. This can include images, videos, music, written content, and even ideas. To protect yourself and your digital marketing efforts, it is crucial to take the following precautions:

1. Familiarize Yourself with Copyright Laws: Take the time to educate yourself about copyright laws in your country or region. Understand the rights of copyright owners and the limitations on use. This knowledge will empower you to make informed decisions and reduce the risk of infringement.

2. Create Original Content: The best way to avoid copyright infringement is to create your own original content. This not only protects you legally but also helps you establish a unique brand identity and stand out from the competition. Strive to be innovative and authentic in your creations.

3. Obtain Proper Licenses: If you wish to use copyrighted material, seek permission from the copyright owner or obtain the necessary licenses. Many platforms offer royalty-free or creative commons-licensed content that can be used with proper attribution. Always give credit where credit is due to respect the rights of others.

4. Conduct Thorough Research: Before using any material, conduct diligent research to determine if it is copyrighted or falls under fair use. Fair use allows limited use of copyrighted material for purposes such as criticism, commentary, news reporting, or educational use. However, fair use is a subjective concept, and it is wise to consult legal experts or utilize online tools to assess the legitimacy of fair use claims.

5. Monitor and Respond to Copyright Claims: Regularly monitor your content for potential copyright claims. If you receive a claim, promptly respond and take appropriate action, such as removing the disputed material or seeking permission. Ignoring copyright claims can lead to legal disputes and damage your reputation.

By adhering to these guidelines, you can navigate the world of digital marketing while respecting copyright laws. Remember, your creativity and originality are your greatest assets. Protect them while building your brand and engaging with your audience.

Disclosures and Transparency in Sponsored Content

Disclosures and Transparency in Sponsored Content

In the fast-paced world of digital marketing, content creators, digital creators, and social media influencers have become powerful players in the game. These individuals have the ability to captivate audiences and drive significant engagement, making them incredibly valuable to brands and businesses. As a content creator in the niche of digital marketing, it is essential to understand the importance of disclosures and transparency when it comes to sponsored content.

Sponsored content refers to any type of content that is created in collaboration with a brand or business in exchange for compensation. This can range from sponsored blog posts and social media posts to sponsored videos and podcasts. While it can be an excellent way for content creators to monetize their platforms, it also comes with a responsibility to maintain transparency and honesty with their audience.

First and foremost, it is crucial to disclose any sponsored content clearly and conspicuously. This means using explicit language like "sponsored," "ad," or "paid partnership" to inform your audience that the content they are consuming is a result of a collaboration with a brand. This disclosure should be placed in a location where it is easily visible and cannot be missed by your audience.

Transparency goes beyond just disclosing the sponsorship; it also involves being honest about your opinions and experiences with the product or service you are promoting. Audiences value authenticity, and they expect content creators to provide them with genuine recommendations. Never endorse a product or service that you do not genuinely support or believe in, as this will erode the trust you have built with your audience.

Another aspect of transparency is maintaining a clear line between sponsored and non-sponsored content. Your audience should be able to distinguish between the two easily. This can be achieved by creating a separate section on your blog or website for sponsored content or using different visual cues, such as a specific background color or logo, to indicate sponsored posts on social media.

Lastly, always remember to comply with the Federal Trade Commission (FTC) guidelines and any other relevant advertising regulations in your country. These guidelines are in place to protect consumers and ensure fair advertising practices. Familiarize yourself with the specific requirements for disclosing sponsored content and stay updated on any changes in the guidelines.

Disclosures and transparency in sponsored content are not only ethical practices but also essential for maintaining a strong and loyal audience. By being upfront about your collaborations and providing honest opinions, you will continue to build trust with your followers, which is invaluable in the world of digital marketing.

Complying with FTC Guidelines

Complying with FTC Guidelines

As a content creator, digital creator, or social media influencer in the digital marketing niche, it is crucial to understand and comply with the guidelines set by the Federal Trade Commission (FTC). These guidelines play a significant role in maintaining transparency, protecting consumers, and ensuring ethical practices within the industry.

The FTC guidelines require that any content created for promotional purposes must be clearly disclosed as advertising. This means that if you are endorsing a product or service, receiving compensation, or have any financial interest in the content you are sharing, you must disclose it to your audience in a transparent manner. Failure to do so can lead to severe consequences, including legal action and damage to your reputation.

To comply with FTC guidelines, it is essential to understand the different methods of disclosure and choose the one that best suits your content and platform. For instance, on social media platforms like Instagram and Twitter, using hashtags such as #ad, #sponsored, or #promotion can help clearly indicate that your post is an advertisement. Similarly, in YouTube videos or blog posts, you can include a disclaimer at the beginning or end of the content, clearly stating your relationship with the product or service being promoted.

It is also crucial to ensure that your disclosures are easily noticeable and understandable to your audience. Disclosures should be placed in a location where they are not easily overlooked and should be presented in a style and language that your audience can easily comprehend. Avoid using vague language or burying the disclosure within a lengthy caption or post.

Moreover, it is important to remember that the responsibility of compliance lies with the content creator, not just the brand or company involved. Even if a brand fails to request disclosure, it is your duty to disclose any relationship or financial interest you have in the content you are creating.

By complying with FTC guidelines, you not only adhere to legal requirements but also build trust and maintain credibility with your audience. Being transparent about your relationships and partnerships can enhance your reputation as an honest and reliable content creator, fostering a loyal following.

In conclusion, understanding and adhering to FTC guidelines is paramount for content creators, digital creators, and social media influencers in the digital marketing niche. By clearly disclosing any financial interests or relationships, you can maintain transparency, protect consumers, and establish yourself as a trustworthy authority in the industry.

Maintaining Authenticity and Trust with Your Audience

Maintaining Authenticity and Trust with Your Audience

In the fast-paced world of digital marketing, maintaining authenticity and trust with your audience is crucial for content creators, digital creators, and social media influencers. In this subchapter, we will delve into the importance of being genuine, building trust, and creating meaningful connections with your audience.

Authenticity is the foundation upon which successful digital marketing campaigns are built. With countless content creators vying for attention, being authentic sets you apart from the noise. Your audience craves realness and relatability. By staying true to yourself, you establish a unique voice and persona that resonates with your followers.

One way to maintain authenticity is by being transparent. Share your journey, your struggles, and your successes. By letting your audience see the real you, they will feel a deeper connection and trust your recommendations. Honesty and transparency foster credibility, which is essential for building trust with your audience.

Trust is the cornerstone of any successful relationship, and the same applies to your relationship with your audience. To gain their trust, consistently provide valuable and reliable content. Deliver on your promises and be consistent in your messaging. When your audience knows they can count on you for quality content, they will trust your recommendations and continue to engage with your brand.

Another effective way to maintain authenticity and trust is by actively engaging with your audience. Building a community around your brand involves listening to your audience's feedback, responding to comments and messages, and genuinely caring about their opinions. By fostering a two-way conversation, you create a sense of community and loyalty.

Furthermore, it is essential to be mindful of the products and services you promote. Only align yourself with brands and products that you truly believe in. Your audience looks up to you for guidance, and promoting something just for the sake of profit can damage your authenticity. Choose partnerships that align with your values and resonate with your audience.

In conclusion, maintaining authenticity and trust with your audience is paramount in the world of digital marketing. By staying true to yourself, being transparent, building trust, and actively engaging with your audience, you create a strong bond that sets you apart from the competition. Remember, authenticity is your superpower, and trust is the currency that will propel your digital marketing success.

Chapter 9: Monetizing Your Digital Presence

Exploring Different Revenue Streams

Exploring Different Revenue Streams

In the ever-evolving digital landscape, content creators, digital creators, and social media influencers need to be adaptable and innovative when it comes to monetizing their creative efforts. While producing high-quality content is crucial, it is equally important to explore diverse revenue streams that can not only sustain your digital marketing efforts but also help you thrive in the competitive world of content creation.

This subchapter of "The Ultimate Guide to Digital Marketing for Content Creators" will delve into various revenue streams that can be leveraged by content creators across different niches, with a specific focus on digital marketing.

1. Sponsored Content: Collaborating with brands and businesses to create sponsored content is a popular revenue stream for content creators. By partnering with relevant brands, you can not only generate income but also expand your audience and increase your credibility.

2. Affiliate Marketing: Affiliate marketing is another powerful way to monetize your digital marketing efforts. By promoting products or services and earning a commission for each sale made through your unique affiliate links, you can generate passive income while providing value to your audience.

3. Digital Products: Create and sell digital products such as e-books, online courses, or exclusive content. This allows you to share your expertise, provide value to your audience, and generate a substantial income stream.

4. Membership or Subscription Model: Offer premium or exclusive content through a membership or subscription model. This not only provides recurring revenue but also fosters a loyal community of supporters who are willing to invest in your content.

5. Crowdfunding: Engage your audience through platforms like Patreon, Kickstarter, or GoFundMe, where they can contribute financially to support your content creation. This funding model allows you to maintain creative control while receiving direct support from your dedicated fan base.

6. Brand Partnerships and Collaborations: Strengthen your online presence and revenue stream by collaborating with other content creators or influencers within your niche. Pooling resources, sharing audiences, and creating joint content can lead to increased visibility and revenue opportunities.

7. Advertisements: Explore advertising opportunities on your website, blog, or social media platforms. Platforms like Google AdSense or sponsored posts on Instagram can provide an additional revenue stream based on ad impressions or clicks.

Remember, integrating multiple revenue streams can diversify your income and provide stability in an ever-changing digital landscape. Experiment with different strategies, evaluate their effectiveness, and adapt accordingly to maximize your earning potential as a content creator in the realm of digital marketing.

Advertising and Sponsorships

Advertising and Sponsorships

In today's digital age, advertising and sponsorships have become an integral part of content creation and digital marketing. As content creators, digital creators, and social media influencers, understanding the dynamics of advertising and sponsorships is crucial to your success in the ever-evolving world of digital marketing.

Advertising is a powerful tool that allows you to promote your content to a wider audience. Whether it's through display ads, social media ads, or sponsored content, advertising helps you reach potential viewers and followers who may not have discovered your content otherwise. It enables you to increase brand awareness, drive traffic to your platforms, and ultimately grow your audience.

When it comes to advertising, it's important to create compelling and engaging ads that resonate with your target audience. Consider your niche and the interests of your followers when crafting your ads. Utilize eye-catching visuals, persuasive copy, and a clear call to action to entice viewers to engage with your content.

Sponsorships, on the other hand, involve partnering with brands or companies that align with your content and values. These partnerships can be mutually beneficial, allowing you to monetize your content while providing the brand with exposure to your audience. Sponsorships can come in various forms, such as product placements, sponsored videos or blog posts, or brand collaborations.

When seeking sponsorships, it's crucial to maintain authenticity and transparency. Choose brands that you genuinely believe in and that align with your audience's interests. Disclose any sponsored content to maintain trust with your followers. Additionally, negotiating fair compensation is important. Consider your reach, engagement, and the value you provide to the brand when discussing financial terms.

As content creators, digital creators, and social media influencers, it's essential to strike a balance between advertising and maintaining the integrity of your content. While advertising and sponsorships can provide financial support and growth opportunities, ensure that your content remains authentic, valuable, and true to your brand.

Furthermore, stay informed about the latest trends and best practices in digital marketing. The world of advertising is constantly evolving, with new platforms, algorithms, and strategies emerging regularly. Stay ahead of the curve by attending industry events, following digital marketing blogs, and networking with other content creators.

By understanding the ins and outs of advertising and sponsorships, you can leverage these opportunities to maximize your reach, monetize your content, and establish yourself as a successful digital creator within the realm of digital marketing.

Creating and Selling Digital Products
Building and Nurturing a Successful Online Community

Building and Nurturing a Successful Online Community

In the world of digital marketing, content creators, digital creators, and social media influencers have a unique advantage when it comes to building and nurturing an online community. With their ability to create compelling content and engage with their audience, they have the power to cultivate a loyal following and drive meaningful connections. This subchapter aims to provide content creators in the niche of digital marketing with valuable insights and strategies to effectively build and nurture a successful online community.

First and foremost, understanding your audience is key to building a thriving community. Take the time to research and identify your target audience's needs, interests, and preferences. By tailoring your content to meet their expectations, you can establish a strong connection and foster a sense of belonging within your community.

Consistency is the backbone of any successful online community. Regularly publishing high-quality, relevant content will not only keep your audience engaged but also attract new members. Utilize various digital marketing techniques such as search engine optimization (SEO) and social media promotion to ensure your content reaches a wider audience.

Engagement is paramount in nurturing an online community. Respond to comments, messages, and inquiries promptly and authentically. Encourage discussions and create a safe space for your community members to share their thoughts and ideas. By actively participating in conversations and valuing your audience's input, you will foster a sense of community and loyalty.

Collaboration is a powerful tool in building and nurturing an online community. Partner with other content creators, digital creators, and social media influencers in your niche to create mutually beneficial relationships. By cross-promoting each other's content and collaborating on projects, you can expand your reach and tap into new audiences.

Creating exclusive content and rewards for your community members can help foster a sense of exclusivity and loyalty. Consider offering exclusive discounts, access to behind-the-scenes content, or even hosting live events or webinars for your most engaged community members. By making them feel special and appreciated, you will strengthen their commitment to your community.

Lastly, continuously analyze and adapt your strategies. Monitor your community's engagement, feedback, and growth metrics to identify what is working and what needs improvement. Stay up-to-date with the latest digital marketing trends and tools to ensure your community remains relevant and thriving.

Building and nurturing a successful online community requires dedication, authenticity, and a deep understanding of your audience. By implementing the strategies outlined in this subchapter, content creators in the niche of digital marketing can cultivate a loyal and engaged online community that will support their growth and success.

Engaging with Your Audience

Providing Value and Building Loyalty

Chapter 10: Conclusion

Recap of Key Digital Marketing Strategies

Highlights of Effective Techniques for Content Creators

Highlights of Effective Techniques for Content Creators

In today's digital age, content creators play a vital role in the world of marketing. Whether you are a blogger, YouTuber, or social media influencer, understanding effective techniques for content creation is crucial to your success. This subchapter will highlight some key strategies that will help you thrive as a content creator in the fast-paced world of digital marketing.

1. Know Your Audience: The first step to creating compelling content is to understand your target audience. Conduct thorough research to identify their interests, pain points, and preferences. This will enable you to tailor your content to meet their needs and keep them engaged.

2. Create High-Quality Content: In a sea of content creators, standing out requires producing high-quality content. Focus on creating valuable and informative content that resonates with your audience. Use high-resolution images, engaging videos, and well-written articles to captivate your viewers.

3. Consistency is Key: Consistency plays a crucial role in building a loyal audience. Develop a content schedule and stick to it. Whether you choose to post daily, weekly, or monthly, ensure that you consistently deliver fresh and engaging content that keeps your audience coming back for more.

4. Optimize for Search Engines: Search engine optimization (SEO) is essential for increasing your content's visibility. Research relevant keywords and incorporate them strategically into your content, titles, and meta descriptions. This will improve your chances of ranking higher in search engine results, driving more traffic to your content.

5. Leverage Social Media: Social media platforms are powerful tools for content creators. Utilize platforms like Instagram, Twitter, and Facebook to promote your content and engage with your audience. Be active, respond to comments, and use hashtags to increase your reach.

6. Collaborate with Others: Collaboration is an effective technique for expanding your audience and reaching new demographics. Partner with other content creators or influencers in your niche to create joint projects or cross-promote each other's content. This will expose your content to a wider audience and help you grow your following.

7. Analyze and Adapt: Regularly analyze your content's performance using analytics tools. Track metrics such as views, engagement, and conversion rates to gain insights into what works and what doesn't. Use this data to adapt your content strategy and improve your future content.

By implementing these effective techniques, content creators can navigate the ever-changing landscape of digital marketing successfully. Remember, knowing your audience, creating high-quality content, being consistent, optimizing for search engines, leveraging social media, collaborating with others, and analyzing and adapting are key to standing out in the world of digital marketing.

Encouragement to Continue Learning and Growing in Digital Marketing

Encouragement to Continue Learning and Growing in Digital Marketing

As content creators, digital creators, and social media influencers, you are already well aware of the power and influence that digital marketing holds in today's ever-evolving digital landscape. The ability to create compelling content and effectively promote it across various online platforms is crucial to your success in reaching and engaging your target audience.

However, in the fast-paced world of digital marketing, it is essential to continuously learn and grow to stay ahead of the competition. Embracing a mindset of lifelong learning will not only enhance your skills and knowledge but also enable you to adapt to the ever-changing trends and technologies in the digital marketing realm.

Digital marketing is a field that is constantly evolving and innovating, with new strategies, tools, and platforms emerging regularly. By staying updated with the latest trends and developments, you can ensure that your content remains fresh, relevant, and resonates with your audience.

One of the key reasons why you should continue learning and growing in digital marketing is to maintain a competitive edge. As content creators, you are vying for the attention of your target audience amidst a sea of online content. By acquiring new skills and knowledge, you can differentiate yourself from the competition and offer unique value to your audience.

Moreover, the digital marketing landscape is highly dynamic, with algorithms changing, new social media platforms emerging, and consumer behaviors evolving. By staying abreast of these changes, you can optimize your content and marketing strategies to effectively reach and engage your audience.

Continuing to learn and grow in digital marketing also opens up new opportunities for monetization and collaboration. As you expand your skillset, you may discover new avenues to generate income, such as offering digital marketing services, partnering with brands, or launching your own products or courses. The more you invest in your digital marketing education, the more opportunities you can create for yourself.

Lastly, learning and growing in digital marketing is not just about acquiring technical knowledge; it also fosters personal and professional growth. By challenging yourself to learn new things, you develop resilience, adaptability, and a growth mindset, which are all essential traits for success in any field.

In conclusion, as content creators, digital creators, and social media influencers, the world of digital marketing offers endless possibilities for growth and success. By embracing a mindset of continuous learning, you can stay ahead of the competition, adapt to the evolving digital landscape, and unlock new opportunities for monetization and collaboration. So, keep learning, keep growing, and watch your digital marketing endeavors flourish.

Final Thoughts and Action Steps

Final Thoughts and Action Steps

Congratulations! You have now reached the final chapter of "The Ultimate Guide to Digital Marketing for Content Creators." Throughout this book, we have covered a wide range of strategies, techniques, and tools to help you excel in the world of digital marketing. As content creators, digital creators, and social media influencers, you hold a unique position in the digital landscape. Your ability to captivate audiences and create engaging content gives you a significant advantage in the realm of digital marketing.

In this final subchapter, we will summarize the key takeaways from this guide and provide you with actionable steps to implement in your digital marketing journey. These steps will enable you to enhance your online presence, grow your audience, and increase your monetization opportunities.

First and foremost, it is crucial to understand your target audience. Take the time to research their demographics, interests, and pain points. By understanding your audience, you can tailor your content and marketing campaigns to resonate with them on a deeper level.

Next, ensure that you have a strong online presence. This includes optimizing your social media profiles, creating a visually appealing website or blog, and consistently producing high-quality content. Remember, consistency is key in the digital world, so establish a content creation schedule and stick to it.

As a content creator, you must leverage various digital marketing channels to promote your content effectively. Experiment with different strategies such as search engine optimization (SEO), email marketing, influencer partnerships, and social media advertising. Monitor the performance of each channel and adjust your strategies accordingly.

Additionally, engage with your audience to build genuine connections. Respond to comments, messages, and feedback promptly. Encourage user-generated content and actively involve your audience in your content creation process. This will not only strengthen your relationship with your followers but also attract new ones through word-of-mouth recommendations.

Lastly, explore monetization opportunities. As a content creator, you have the potential to generate income through sponsored content, affiliate marketing, brand collaborations, merchandise sales, and more. However, be cautious about maintaining the authenticity and integrity of your content. Only partner with brands and products that align with your values and resonate with your audience.

In conclusion, as a content creator, digital creator, or social media influencer, digital marketing is an invaluable tool that can significantly enhance your online presence and success. By implementing the action steps outlined in this subchapter, you can take your digital marketing strategies to the next level and achieve your goals. Remember, the digital landscape is ever-evolving, so continue to stay informed, adapt to changes, and consistently deliver exceptional content to your audience. Best of luck on your digital marketing journey!

Implementing Strategies Learned in the Book

Implementing Strategies Learned in the Book

Congratulations! You have just completed reading "The Ultimate Guide to Digital Marketing for Content Creators," and you are now equipped with a wealth of knowledge to take your content creation and digital presence to the next level. This subchapter will help you understand how to implement the strategies learned in the book and unleash your full potential as a content creator, digital creator, or social media influencer in the dynamic world of digital marketing.

The first step in implementing the strategies is to assess your current digital marketing efforts. Take a moment to evaluate your existing content and social media channels. Identify areas where you can improve and align them with the strategies outlined in the book. This may involve creating a content calendar, optimizing your website for search engines, or revamping your social media profiles.

With your assessment complete, it's time to dive into action. Start by prioritizing the strategies that resonate most with your niche and goals. Remember, not all strategies may be applicable to your specific digital marketing needs, so focus on those that align with your audience and content.

One of the key takeaways from the book is the importance of creating engaging and valuable content. Implement this strategy by conducting thorough research on your target audience's preferences, pain points, and interests. Craft content that resonates with them and brings value to their lives. Whether it's through blog posts, videos, podcasts, or social media posts, make sure your content is informative, entertaining, and shareable.

Another strategy highlighted in the book is the power of social media marketing. Implement this by developing a strong social media presence on platforms that your target audience frequents. Create a content calendar and schedule regular posts to maintain consistency. Engage with your audience by responding to comments, messages, and mentions promptly. Collaborate with fellow content creators, influencers, and brands to expand your reach and amplify your message.

Additionally, the book emphasizes the importance of measuring and analyzing your digital marketing efforts. Implement this strategy by tracking key performance indicators (KPIs) such as website traffic, social media engagement, conversion rates, and audience demographics. Utilize analytics tools to gain insights into your audience's behavior and preferences, allowing you to refine your strategies further.

In conclusion, implementing the strategies learned in "The Ultimate Guide to Digital Marketing for Content Creators" requires a combination of research, planning, and consistent execution. By understanding your audience, creating valuable content, leveraging social media, and analyzing your efforts, you can propel your digital marketing efforts to new heights. Embrace the knowledge gained from this book, adapt it to your niche, and watch your digital presence flourish. Good luck on your digital marketing journey!

Inspiring Content Creators to Thrive in the Digital Marketing Landscape

Inspiring Content Creators to Thrive in the Digital Marketing Landscape

In today's fast-paced digital world, content creators have become the driving force behind successful marketing campaigns. Whether you're a blogger, vlogger, podcaster, or social media influencer, the power of digital marketing cannot be underestimated. This subchapter aims to inspire content creators to embrace the digital marketing landscape and empower them to thrive in their respective niches.

As a content creator, you have a unique opportunity to connect with your audience and build a loyal following. Digital marketing provides you with a plethora of tools and strategies to amplify your content, reach a wider audience, and ultimately achieve your goals. This subchapter will guide you through the essential steps to leverage digital marketing effectively and elevate your content creation game.

First and foremost, understanding the fundamentals of digital marketing is crucial. This includes grasping concepts such as SEO, social media marketing, email marketing, and content distribution. By familiarizing yourself with these principles, you can develop a comprehensive digital marketing strategy tailored to your niche and target audience.

Next, we delve into the importance of creating compelling and engaging content. In the digital marketing landscape, content is king. You'll learn how to craft content that resonates with your audience, evokes emotion, and leaves a lasting impact. We'll provide you with tips and tricks to optimize your content for search engines, increase your visibility, and drive organic traffic to your platforms.

Furthermore, we'll explore the power of social media and how it can be harnessed to boost your digital presence. From Instagram to YouTube, we'll discuss the best practices for each platform and how to leverage them to grow your audience, build your brand, and monetize your content effectively.

Additionally, this subchapter will shed light on the importance of data analytics and tracking the performance of your digital marketing efforts. By analyzing metrics and insights, you can gain valuable information about your audience's preferences, behaviors, and demographics. This data can then be used to optimize your content and tailor your marketing strategies accordingly.

To inspire and motivate you, we'll also feature success stories from renowned content creators who have thrived in the digital marketing landscape. Their journeys will serve as a beacon of hope, demonstrating that with dedication, creativity, and a solid digital marketing strategy, you too can achieve your goals and make a lasting impact in your niche.

In conclusion, this subchapter aims to inspire and empower content creators, digital creators, and social media influencers to thrive in the ever-evolving digital marketing landscape. By understanding the fundamental principles, creating compelling content, harnessing the power of social media, analyzing data, and drawing inspiration from success stories, you can take your content creation endeavors to new heights and achieve the recognition and success you deserve.

Made in the USA
Monee, IL
27 August 2023

41679055R00079